THE ROAD TO VICHY
1918 - 1938

By the same author

Introduction à l'ontologie du connaître, *Desclée De Brouwer, Paris,* 1934.

Critique de la connaissance morale, *Desclée De Brouwer, Paris,* 1934.

La campagne d'Ethiopie et la pensée politique française, *Desclée De Brouwer, Paris,* 1936.

Trois leçons sur le travail, *Téqui, Paris,* 1938.

Nature and Functions of Authority, *Marquette University Press, Milwaukee, Wisconsin,* 1940.

THE ROAD TO VICHY
1918-1938

by

YVES R. SIMON

Translated by
JAMES A. CORBETT *and*
GEORGE J. McMORROW

NEW YORK
SHEED & WARD
1942

COPYRIGHT, 1942
BY SHEED & WARD, INC.

MANUFACTURED IN THE UNITED STATES OF AMERICA
BY THE HADDON CRAFTSMEN, INC., CAMDEN, N. J.

To the memory of my brother

JEAN SIMON

who died on the field of honor
April 14, 1917

CONTENTS

I.	France under the Swastika	1
II.	The Aftermath of the Victory	10
III.	Nationalism and Pacifism	32
IV.	Politics and Religion	53
V.	The Twilight of the Myths	79
VI.	Our Friends' Friends Are Our Friends	99
VII.	The People's Front in Power	118
VIII.	Our Enemies' Enemies Are Our Friends	147
IX.	What Is a Traitor?	178
X.	The Deliverance of the World	195

THE ROAD TO VICHY
1918 - 1938

I

France under the Swastika

Let us never speak of France without keeping in mind the new political map of French territory. The occupied area embraces Alsace, Lorraine, Flanders and Artois, Paris, Normandy, Beauce and Brittany, the Charentes, Bordeaux, the entire Channel and Atlantic coast, all the agricultural regions of major importance and most of the industrial centers. One million, five hundred thousand young Frenchmen are prisoners of war. Famine rages everywhere. Needless to say, censorship is rigorous. This whole picture brings to mind that on the day following the Armistice, the Nazi radio declared that henceforth the lot of the French would be one of work, silence, and absolute obedience.

France is no longer a Republic. It is true that the French State is still spoken of in official acts, but on some new postcards you read simply: *France,* that glorious name which can signify a mere geographical unit as well as a state. The Nazis could have occupied the whole of France, and named a governor-general. They judged it preferable to sign an agreement with a Marshal of France. Their military force, supported by the weapon of hunger, assured them the mastery of the situation in any eventuality. All of France is held hostage. All of France is accountable to the Nazis for the actions of the Vichy government.

The Battle of France has been lost, but the Battle of the World goes on, and will be won. For the peoples still engaged in the struggle, it is of the utmost importance to understand the historical significance of the government which claims to represent France today. We want to know, and the world ought to know, whence it comes and where it is going: things that certain followers of that government, in the astonishment of the disaster, might very well not have understood.

Marshal Pétain was brought into power in order to apply for an armistice from Hitler. Why did the most ignominious capitulation in French history have to be signed by a Marshal of France? On the French side, it is quite possible that certain naïve people, thinking they were still living in the time of imperial Germany, and incapable of realizing the difference between the heads of a plebeian revolution and the soldiers of the House of Hohenzollern, believed that the prestige of the hero of Verdun would assure France an honorable treatment. As a matter of fact, nothing was saved, not even honor, for a Marshal of France promised (article 19 of the Armistice Convention) to deliver on demand to the Nazi executioners the German refugees who had put their confidence in French hospitality. Some of them had in the meantime fought in the French army against the common enemy of the French people and of the German people. But let us imagine that the Armistice, instead of being signed by Marshal Pétain, had been signed by some ordinary politician. It would not have been possible, then, to tell the French people that accepting the Nazi victory was a patriotic duty. The Free French Forces today would be ten times more powerful than they actually are. The French Empire would have continued or resumed the struggle on the side of Great Britain; the Fascist army in Africa and the Fascist navy would have been rapidly annihilated; there would never have been a German army in Libya, nor Nazi agents at Dakar,—that indispensable base for an attack upon the New World. From the Nazi viewpoint, such consequences had to be avoided at any cost. *Is fecit cui prodest!* Hitler would never have succeeded in establishing his control over the German people, had his ambiguous personality not been sponsored by two men able to pacify even those who felt the greatest disgust. These men were the venerable Marshal von Hindenburg, eighty years old, the conqueror of Tannenberg and a national hero, and the Catholic von Papen, one-time organizer of sabotage in the United States and a redoubtable enemy of Communism. Similarly, it was surely advantageous for Hitler to have his victory over France solemnly recognized by Marshal Pétain, the saviour of Verdun.

About a year ago, an admirer of the Vichy government declared to the American people that the "philosophy" of the "New French Regime" was the antithesis of Nazism.[1] He should have concluded that the "New Regime" will never be given the slightest chance of applying its philosophy so long as the Nazis dominate France and Europe. For the Nazis are stubborn in their philo-

---

[1] L. J. A. Mercier, *The New French Regime*, The Commonweal, March 7, 1941.

sophical convictions, and they are not accustomed to tolerate philosophies opposed to their own, except in the indispensable periods of transition. On the other hand, it is evident to the entire world that the defeat of the Nazis will entail the immediate overthrow of the government born of the catastrophe of the French army. *The men of Vichy have cast their lot with the defeat of the Allies.* Marshal Pétain invites the French people to collaborate with their conquerors: we know what sort of collaboration their conquerors are exacting from them. Maybe there were, among the early supporters of the Vichy government, some mistaken patriots. Would they be willing to accept a national liberation which would include the inglorious liquidation of their "regime" and the coming of the Fourth French Republic? They doubtlessly prefer to foster within themselves the hope that Nazi Germany, after having defeated Great Britain and subdued the New World, will magnanimously renounce her conquests and permit France to become a free nation once more.

But Frenchmen whom no party spirit compels to cherish such criminal fantasies, understood long ago that the deliverance of France, and the deliverance of all the enslaved peoples, absolutely depend on a British and American victory. They realized long ago that all propaganda in favor of the "New French Regime" is propaganda against the United States and Great Britain.

What is this so-called "New French Regime" whose survival is possible only because of the tolerant protection of the enemies of France? Does it make sense to speak of a French Regime in the present state of France, when the enemy is at Paris, Brest, Bordeaux; when the youth of France is a prisoner of war; when famine is everywhere? The government of Marshal Pétain is a political form of transition, destined to make possible the complete control of the international Nazis over the French people.

Whoever has followed French political life in the past few years knows very well that when the war broke out, there were in France a certain number of powerful people for whom nothing was more important than the destruction of democratic liberties and the establishment of a gang-dictatorship after the Fascist or Nazi pattern. These people passed themselves off as nationalists (a word which will soon be synonymous with traitor). As a matter of fact, most of them came from the part of French society where the Nationalist party traditionally recruited its adherents. Were they conscious of betraying their country? The fact is that before the war, during the war and ever since the Armistice, their policy has been one of treachery. They have been the more or less unconscious instruments of Hitler: rather than see the victory of Britain and America and the restoration of the French Republic, they are ready to become—nay, they have already become his conscious instruments. They could not assume power right after the defeat of France, for the French people would have treated them as so many Quislings and perhaps made them powerless. Patriots had to be reassured. A period of transition was necessary. A compromise was necessary. In order to carry out their plans effectively, the French partisans of the dictators needed a man whose name was a symbol of patriotism. They needed a conservative. They needed a Catholic. Moreover the advanced age of Marshal Pétain assured them that the period of transition would not be too long.

There are great Frenchmen living in France today who have realized admirably that their task is to work within the limits of the existing compromise in order to save whatever can be saved of France. In the face of certain infamies, and in spite of censorship and propaganda, they are keeping alive the flames of French honor and of republican spirit. They try, through hard work and mutual help, to keep children from dying of hunger. Their charity is holding in check the powers of despair, their love of truth is holding in check the powers of deception.

As for the French living in free countries, their place is alongside the Allied forces. The Frenchmen in France, who are serving the common cause in the darkness of capitulation, are their brothers in arms, and know it very well. Among Frenchmen, there is only one division which matters today: that into those who serve their country and those who betray it.

Why is not the writer of these pages somewhere in Africa, under the flag of the Cross of Lorraine? Grave infirmities prevent me from being a soldier. My home is among those whom no mobilization has divided, whom famine has not invaded. But to avoid the disgrace of not serving at all, I wish to offer this contribution, however feeble it may be, to the explanation of our time: for the deliverance of the world depends upon the understanding of the history that we are living.

The following pages are for the most part an exposition of my observations on the political life of France from 1918 to 1938. I trust that these observations, by calling attention to certain aspects not sufficiently known of the history of contemporary France, will help many minds to overcome the dismal confusion caused by this bewildering event, the sudden fall of the French Republic. Understanding the defeat of yesterday is necessary to assure the victory of tomorrow. The powers which brought about the fall of France are still at work all over the world. Propaganda uses the same tricks, exploits the same passions, the same uncertainties, the same scruples, the same ignorance. The Trojan Horse is still trying to pass itself off as a tutelary deity.

II

The Aftermath of the Victory

IN 1918 I was fifteen years old. On the day of the Armistice our teachers were quite disposed to hold their classes as usual. But apparently they were afraid that history would not forgive them for having failed to celebrate such a day. We crossed the town in mournful ranks. On my return home, I listened to my mother reading a letter from a friend: "I am thinking especially of you on this day, which is for you one of great sorrow." During the preceding weeks, I had noticed with a childlike astonishment that my mother showed little interest in the events which were pointing to victory:

the capitulations of Bulgaria, Turkey and Austria-Hungary. My brother, a volunteer, had been killed in the war. I realized on that November 11th that the mothers whose sons had been killed did not want to be consoled. I now realize that France did not want to be consoled either. She had had too many sons killed in the war. And, while an exceptional clear-sightedness was needed to overcome the tremendous difficulties which the establishment of peace involved, confusion, doubt and resentment developed in all parts of French society. The trial had been too severe and something essential had given way. Our youth was beginning in an atmosphere of disillusionment. Many of us were to be easy prey for the worst forces of destruction: skepticism, cynicism and despair.

But what was this *something essential* that the excess of suffering had destroyed in the heart of the French nation? Twenty years later I thought I understood what it was, as I re-read certain pages of Charles Péguy. To those who were already scoffing at the Republic, Péguy replied:

"You are forgetting, you are ignoring that there has been a Republican mysticism, and though you forget and ignore it, it will not be as if it had not been. Men have died for freedom just as men have died for the Faith. These elections today seem to you a ridiculous formality, universally deceitful and altogether crooked, and you have the right to say so. But men have lived, countless men, heroes, martyrs, and I shall even say saints—and when I say saints I believe I know whereof I speak—countless men have lived heroic, saintly lives; men have suffered, men have died, a whole people has lived so that any fool today may have the right to go through this crooked formality. It was a terrible, a hard, a formidable travail. It was not always utterly ridiculous. And peoples around us, whole peoples, races, labor in the same painful travail, work and struggle to obtain this laughable formality. These elections are laughable. But there was a time, my dear Variot,[2] an heroic time when the sick and the dying had themselves carried in their chairs *to cast their votes*. To cast your vote: today this expression seems to you utterly ridiculous. Yet it was prepared by a century of heroism. And I do not mean fake heroism, literary heroism. It was prepared by a century of the most unquestionable, of the most genuine heroism, and I will say of the most *French* heroism. These elections are laughable. But there has been one election. It

---

[2] Jean Variot, author of various political and sociological essays, was a collaborator with Péguy.

was the great division of the world, the great choice that the modern world had to make between the Ancien Régime and the Revolution. It was a famous contest, Variot, Jean Variot. Think of this little contest which began at the mill of Valmy[3] and which scarcely came to an end on the heights of Hougoumont . . ."[4]

And which scarcely came to an end: the spirit of the French Revolution did not cease to live after Waterloo. Charles Péguy does not specify the date of its disappearance; in fact this spirit was still alive at the time Péguy wrote. The spirit of the French Revolution survived the defeat of Napoleon by more than a century. It blew upon the entire world during the first World War. It conquered, and then died out on November 11th without anyone being aware of what was happening. THE FRENCH REVOLUTION? 1789-1918.

I hate as much as any man the numerous and monstrous errors of the French revolutionary tradition. I am not one of those Catholics whom the *Syllabus* of Pius IX embarrasses. Yet it is a fact that the end of the revolutionary spirit left France

---

[3] Valmy was the scene of the first victory of the armies of the French Revolution against the invaders (Sept. 20, 1792); Hougoumont was a strategic position on the battlefield of Waterloo.

[4] Charles Péguy, *Notre Jeunesse*, Paris, Gallimard, p. 26. First published in 1910.

disabled, and her friends abandoned her one after another, for France had lost the inspiring idea by which she had been recognized, because of which she had been loved and hated for nearly a century and a half. There were so many grave errors in the French revolutionary tradition that the end of this tradition may have been considered a purification. It would have been a real and a priceless purification if a greater and purer idea had taken the place of the revolutionary idea. In fact, no other idea sprang up. The place left void by the disappearance of the revolutionary idea remained empty, and the void thus produced has exhausted France.

The worship of liberty, justice and right was in many ways an idolatrous one: it was also a homage paid to the *unknown God*, for liberty and justice are names of the true God. The collapse of revolutionary beliefs gave practical atheism an unexpected opportunity. Soon Mussolini will speak of the rotten corpse of the goddess of liberty: many people will not make any distinction between the rotten corpse and the Divine Name. The Divine Name will be scoffed at more surely than the goddess whom our fathers adored. And, again, from Péguy:

"Immediately after us begins the world which

THE AFTERMATH OF THE VICTORY

we have called and will not cease to call the modern world. The world which thinks it is so smart. The world of the clever, of those who believe they are up-to-date, of those who do not want to be given lessons, of those who do not want to be taken in. It is the world of those who no longer have anything to be taught. The world of those who think they are so smart. It is the world of those who are not dupes and fools like ourselves. That is to say, the world of those who believe in nothing, not even in atheism. The movement of the *derepublicanization* of France is fundamentally the same movement as that of her *dechristianization*."[5] At the end of the movement described by Péguy, there will be the *realistic little cads* of whom Bernanos speaks,—readers of *Le Jour*, of *Candide*, of *Gringoire*, of *Je Suis Partout*, insulters of the oppressed and lovers of force. These scoundrels were truly atheists, even though they went to mass. Whoever mocks these divine names, liberty, justice, mercy, cannot remain a worshipper of the true God.

Nothing is more important for the understanding of later developments than the state of French opinion in the years immediately following the war. Before attempting a description of it, how-

[5] *ibid.*, p. 14.

ever, it is necessary to define the portion of French society with which my observations are chiefly concerned.

By birth I belong to the Catholic section of the middle bourgeoisie. What does this class, or this section of a class, represent in the national life as a whole? To give an idea of its importance, it is sufficient to mention that it furnishes or at least incorporates a large part of the officers of both the Army and the Navy, a large part of the clergy and of the legal profession, many industrialists, many doctors, most of the conservative politicians, many high school and university teachers. From it are drawn the admirers of the French Academy, the readers of the "pious" newspapers and of the *Revue des Deux Mondes*. The Catholic middle bourgeoisie mingles occasionally with the upper industrial and financial bourgeoisie, and more regularly with the conservative aristocracy. In some regions it makes common cause with the landowning farmers; the village notary and the farmer often agree to throw the blame for their troubles upon the grammar-school teacher notorious for his so-called advanced ideas, the Leftist politician, and the socialist workingman.

The Catholic middle class had taken an enormous part in the sacrifices of the Great War. In spite of frightful losses, it had kept to the end a magnificent spirit of patriotic resolution. It had upheld Clémenceau without reservation, an extremely significant fact. Does anyone still remember who Clémenceau was before he became the organizer of victory? No Leftist politician had aroused more anger and contempt among the Catholic bourgeoisie. He was a man of many hates and of few friends. An irreconcilable enemy of the Church, a militant atheist, he had played a major role in the antireligious campaigns of the preceding years. He had been the most determined defender of Dreyfus, and the sponsor of Emile Zola in his polemics against the General Staff. For many reasons, he was odious to Catholic circles and to the Catholic bourgeoisie in particular. But in 1917 Clémenceau became the incarnation of the will to conquer. He was the ruthless adversary of the defeatists, of those who favored a negotiated peace, of the irresolute and of the traitors. The Socialist Party sat in the opposition. Clémenceau's appeal echoed the voice of Danton, and the entire nation responded. Catholics supported him wholeheartedly in his policy for victory; thinking sometimes of his past anti-religious struggles, they simply prayed for his conversion.

Ideological motives had little to do with this

magnificently patriotic conduct. Very simple sentiments, springing from the national tradition and ceaselessly stimulated by every manifestation of national life, sufficed to solve all problems. Every bomb dropped on Paris meant one more reason to conquer. That was all, and the war was won.

But soon after the victory, sentiments lost something of their heroic coloring. This, no doubt, was quite natural. Enthusiasm gave way to blind and blinding passions. The spirit of self-seeking supplanted the spirit of sacrifice. Everybody started to argue, and since information was almost totally lacking, it was inevitable that so many arguments should lead to worthless simplifications. The nation under arms had had familiar watchwords, which were true inasmuch as they were simply the expression of a collective will devoted to national salvation. When the tension of the public will had been relaxed—that is, as soon as the victory had become a fact—, slogans were substituted for watchwords, and public opinion found itself fettered by formulas elaborated under deplorable conditions of ignorance, agitation and rancor. Let us examine some of the beliefs crystallized in these slogans.

Above all, there was a general belief in the exclusive guilt of Germany. *Germany, and Germany alone wanted the war:* this was the first of the slogans which took the place of political thinking in that portion of French society with which my observations are principally concerned. This did not mean that the allies of Germany had no responsibility in the catastrophe, but little attention was paid to the complicated stories of the conflicts between the Austro-Hungarian Empire and the Southern Slavs. No one suspected that the imperialism of the Czars, protectors of the Southern Slavs and rivals of Austria-Hungary, had played a major role in the developments leading to the war. Finally, it never occurred to anyone that the policy of the French government could have contributed in any way to the situation from which the war arose. Everyone realized that, in order to establish a solid peace, it was indispensable to understand the causes of the recent war, but by way of explanation they were satisfied with an item of propaganda easy to grasp and easy to exploit.

The nation which was judged solely guilty of unleashing the war was further accused of having conducted it with unprecedented ferocity. Propaganda has no doubt exaggerated the crimes committed by the German armies (from 1914 to 1918 we were fed stories of chopped off hands, and of poisoned candy dropped over the towns by German aviators), yet it is unquestionable that a fair number of German atrocities were only too real. I am thinking above all of the massacres of civilians in Belgium and of the systematic devastation of Northern France. The persistent anger of the French people against such horror was only too well founded. In the French state of mind, the false and dangerous idea was that all those crimes were entirely unprecedented, that no other people in the world had ever been guilty of such horror, that no other people in the world had ever equalled or would be able to equal the cruelty of the German people. This was an historical error and the educated youth soon realized it. We soon heard of the methods used by the Conquistadors in the New World, of the manner in which the civil wars of the French Revolution were conducted, and of Napoleon's Spanish war. Since then we have closely watched another Spanish war. . . .

But during these first years after the War, it was an unquestioned dogma that the German soil had produced an historically unique monster of perfidy and ferocity. To the Germans was applied the notion of "criminal race." This confused and oversimple notion gratifies primitive intellects because of its very simplicity and confusion. What will be the "criminal race" of to-morrow? Today the Jews are the criminal race; in 1919 it was the Germans. "He has German blood in his veins" was said then as today some would say: "He has Jewish blood." To apply to a people the notion of criminal race amounts to extending to it a general Law of Suspects. In equity, an innocent man has never to give proof of his innocence; the burden of the proof rests upon the accuser. But according to the Law of Suspects every member of the suspected group has to give proof of his innocence; otherwise he is treated as guilty. Such is the condition of the Jews in enslaved Europe today. Such was the condition of the Germans in the eyes of the French bourgeoisie in the first years of the postwar period. Catholic, democrat or socialist, it made no difference: it was understood that every German was an accomplice of the Kaiser and of the torturers of Belgium. The Law of Suspects was applied with such passion that the innocent person was left no means of proving his innocence. Even the sacrifice of one's life was not always judged sufficient, and when Erzberger, a Catholic and a democrat, fell under the bullets of the German nationalists, Léon Daudet told the readers of *L'Action Française* that they had reason to rejoice, for it meant "one less German."

In 1814 and 1815 Metternich took care to facilitate the task of the King of France who had been restored to his rights by the Allied victory. In the restored Monarchy, he rightly saw a guarantee against the turbulent spirit of revolutionary and Napoleonic France. Why did not the French in 1919 likewise try to strengthen the precarious situation of democracy in Germany? The answer is found in the slogan, indefatigably repeated in France during the fourteen years of the German Republic: *Republic or monarchy, Germany is always Germany*. The Law of Suspects admitted of no exception.

To increase the confusion, the idea that the German people were an all-powerful race was associated with the idea that they were a criminal race. In the preceding generations and during the four years of the Great War, Germany had certainly given brilliant proofs of her strength. This strength was strangely magnified in the imagination of the French bourgeois. During the whole war he had pictured the German nation as a marvelously homogeneous and well-disciplined unit, in which millions of ingenious minds and strong bodies were working in perfect harmony for the triumph of a bad cause. If some evidence of indiscipline or incompetence was found in the French army, the bourgeois at once shook his head and remarked that such a thing would not be tolerated in Germany. If the French Parliament hampered the government's work, he hastened to praise the superiority of Prussian autocracy. Any strike in France provoked the remark that there were certainly no strikes in Germany. We learned later that in Germany also there had been incompetence, intrigues, political obstructionism and finally mutinies which were serious enough to precipitate the fall of the Empire. These facts never received much publicity in France.

Numerous Germans refused to admit that Germany had been defeated; on the other hand, numerous Frenchmen soon persuaded themselves that, owing to a fatal imprudence of Marshal Foch, Germany had withdrawn from the war with her forces intact, and that she would soon undertake a new aggression. Even if the French statesmen were aware of the real situation in Germany, they could hardly avoid being influenced by the prevailing belief that the military power of Germany was still a formidable menace.

This hatred and this fear of Germany were combined with a bitter resentment toward certain Frenchmen. While it was considered obvious that no Frenchman had wanted war, it was also considered obvious that war could not have occurred if the national defence had not been jeopardized by bad politics. In 1914, France was far less prepared for war than Germany; this fact was not debatable. The lack of heavy artillery and the lack of machine guns had cost the lives of countless Frenchmen. It was natural, and to some extent perfectly just, to place the blame on the parties which had opposed measures for military preparation. But, as soon as party-spirit comes into play, the most justified criticisms become a systematic exploitation of the adversary's faults. Party-spirit did come into play.

In connection with the Dreyfus case, numerous Liberal[6] politicians had participated in violent attacks against the army and its chiefs. The Socialists had wildly indulged in anti-militaristic campaigns; some Socialists were openly anti-patriotic; even those who, like Jaurès, remained patriots, had encouraged imprudent measures of disarmament and cherished illusions as to what would be the action of the German proletariat in favor of peace. The declarations made by international socialist organizations had greatly disturbed French military and political leaders. If the international leaders of the

---

[6] The French word *radical* is not properly translated by the English word radical. We use the word Liberal throughout this book in reference to the *Parti radical* as the closest approximation.

working class were not overrating their power, the organized proletariat would answer the order for general mobilization by calling a general strike, and then, according to the warning of Jules Guesde, the most socialistic country would be crushed. Many people feared that this country might be France. In fact, as soon as war appeared inevitable, national unity prevailed all over Europe and the mobilization, in France as well as in Germany, took place in perfect order. But the impression that France had had a narrow escape persisted. Soon it was learned that the German Socialist representatives had almost unanimously voted the war appropriations. The French Socialists had done the same. It was exceedingly tempting to pass this over in silence, while constantly focusing attention on the German vote. There was a story current that the German Socialists had been the conscious agents of the Kaiser, that one of them, Hermann Müller, had been sent to Paris on the eve of the war by the General Staff for the purpose of undermining the morale of his French comrades. If we consider, furthermore, that a member of the Catholic bourgeoisie sees little difference between a Liberal politician and a Socialist politician, we have a set of images of incomparable value for publicity and election campaigns: there would not have been any war if France had been well armed; in 1914 France was poorly armed because the Liberals (and the Socialists, who were agitating in the background) had, for demagogical reasons, neglected or even opposed the necessary preparations; *France was invaded because the French had voted unwisely*. They voted for Liberals who were more interested in anti-clerical action than in national defence; they voted for utopian-minded Socialists, pacifists and illusionists who trusted the words of their "German brothers" and allowed themselves to be fooled by these "brothers" in the service of the Kaiser. To prevent a new invasion, the first thing to do was to vote rightly, that is to vote for the Right, against the Liberals and the Socialists.

All this seemed very clear, and, apart from some exaggerations and calumnies,[7] quite reasonable. Yet, under the appearance of clarity and reason, a formidable factor of confusion found its way into French politics. The supreme electoral argument of the Rightist parties was that their adversaries had proved incapable of coping with the German

[7] It is not doubtful that the German General Staff regarded favorably the campaigns of the French Socialists for disarmament. But it has never been proved that the German Socialists played the machiavellian role of conscious tools of German militarism. In particular the story of the mission given to Hermann Müller by the German General Staff is a fiction invented for the purposes of propaganda.

danger. The political destiny of the Rightist parties was bound up with the existence of a threat of invasion. If an understanding between France and Germany should be firmly established; if an efficacious organization for collective security should be realized; if a real and lasting disarmament of Germany should take place, the French Right would lose the best item of its propaganda. The politicians of the French Right considered themselves as the guardians of the city, and it is especially in this capacity that they claimed honor and power. It was necessary, then, that the city be, or at least believe herself to be, under the constant menace of a powerful and wicked enemy. It was necessary to circulate the idea that Germany had never disarmed, or that she had quickly rearmed. It was necessary to make the French believe that the socialistic and Catholic governments of Germany were as imperialistic as the generals of the Kaiser. Every German gesture of good will would have to break against a wall of distrust. Every German statesman sincerely desirous of establishing peaceful relations with France (and certainly there were some) would have to be likened to the wolf in the fable who came in sheep's clothing. The international institutions intended to guarantee peace would have to be characterized as "pacifistic dreams," identified with the illusions preceding 1914 and undermined by scorn before being disabled by treason.

Fourteen years later, a day came when really bloodthirsty men took over Germany. The German rearmament was about to become something serious. Then, a man who was a typical representative of the Catholic middle bourgeoisie said to me: "It is better this way; the issue will be clearer and we shall have less chance of being fooled." Between the Third Reich of Hitler and the Republic of Wirth and Stresemann, the essential difference seemed to him to be that between a clear situation and a confused one. A clear situation is always better than a confused one. It was said that Germany was about to start an all-out rearmament: but unless you questioned the slogans which you had been fed for fourteen years, she had never done anything else during those fourteen years. Nothing essential had been changed. There was therefore no particular reason for alarm. The policy of the know-it-alls, of those who pretended to be clear-sighted, of those who did not want to be fooled by the German pacifists, was to make a large number of Frenchmen blind to the change which took place the day Hitler's dictatorship was established in Germany. They did not want to be fooled by Stresemann, and they would be fooled by Hitler. The myth of "eternal Germany" hid the face of the New Germany.

Not to be fooled! Yet this was the major concern of those know-it-alls whose character Péguy described with so much insight ("those who do not want to be given lessons . . . those who do not want to be taken in . . . those who are not dupes and fools. . . "). Among the slogans which they hammered into our minds during the first postwar years, the most vulgar is not the least typical: *Frenchmen are suckers*. Under the cover of a campaign for the defence of the vital interests of France, they started a campaign against all the generous sentiments which formed the very soul of France and the very essence of her historical vocation. Undoubtedly, the French nation has often, in the course of her history, been guilty of selfishness, just as each one of us in his everyday life sins against the ten commandments written in his heart. But everyone knows what a difference there is between a sinner who keeps the sense of virtue alive within himself, and the dead soul into which the light of virtue can no longer penetrate. The France of old and the France of the Revolution had preserved an ideal of generosity amidst numerous faults. "Dechristianization and derepublicanization" as Péguy called it: following the

Great War, with the spirit of the French Revolution asleep, a gang of cynics threw themselves upon France and undertook the systematic extinction of every spark of idealism which was still alive within her. The expression "really French," which until recently had a glorious meaning, came to have a debasing connotation. A "really French" feeling, in the language of the cynics, was a feeling worthy of a sucker. Respect for the conquered? a really French feeling. Sympathy for the weak? a really French feeling. Forgiveness? a really French feeling. The spirit of chivalrous daring? of all really French feelings, the one which prompted the most sarcasm. Fidelity to the pledged word? Hospitality? Finally, the idea that a law of justice ought to outweigh the possibilities of force, in international life as well as in other human relations? All these were really French feelings in place of which it was imperative that the harshness of the "sacro egoismo" be substituted. But how explain that the French people tolerated the preaching of a deadly doctrine, so obviously opposed to the very heart of the French tradition? Here, it is particularly important to keep in mind the state of exhaustion in which victory had left France. Georges Bernanos said of the treaty of Munich that it was a "miscarriage of France, raped by scoundrels while she slept in the woods." Scoundrels succeeded in raping France, because she had fallen asleep from exhaustion after four years of gigantic efforts.

The policy recommended by the disparagers of *really French feelings* called itself a nationalistic policy,—an equivocal and very hypocritical expression. Its true name is isolationism. The egoist practices isolation: this is logical. Then a day comes when he sees around him only a death-like solitude: this is equally logical. For twenty years, nationalists repeated to the French people that their role was not to make justice reign in the world, but to mind their own business. And on a fatal day, France found herself alone, and she collapsed before the enemy, after putting her signature on a scrap of paper on which you could surely find nothing that is *really French*.

III
Nationalism and Pacifism

In 1920, I left my family and my province to study at the University in Paris. Most of my fellow students were more or less engaged in political movements. I did not imitate those who spent most of their time in committee meetings and noisy demonstrations. Yet, I was interested in politics and observed attentively what was going on around me.

I realized that the big issue was not the question of the internal regime, nor that of social and economic organization. International peace was the foremost problem. I cannot recall without emotion the anguish I experienced then while looking at the map of Europe, still overwhelmed as I was by the war which had cost the lives of so many dear ones. It was the time when peace-loving men in Germany were falling before the bullets of those who were going to become the Nazis. These assassinations proved without any doubt that genuine forces of peace were at work in Germany; they also proved that forces of revenge were active and ready to stop at nothing. It seemed clear to me that the forces of revenge would one day get the upper hand unless something were done to bring about a new situation.

Once the Allies had won the war, the solution of the problem of French security could be sought in three directions: territorial dispositions, collective assistance, permanent military superiority. Finally, these three systems might be combined to some extent.

The first system was recommended by the groups of the extreme Right. The most audacious ones demanded the destruction of German unity. It seems that this possibility was never seriously contemplated by French statesmen. What Clémenceau, president of the Council, and Poincaré, President of the Republic (strongly supported by Marshal Foch) asked for, was the permanent occupation of a line of fortresses on the Rhine. They did not plan an annexation properly so-called, but rather the creation of a new military frontier, coupled with political autonomy for the Rhineland. The determined opposition of the British and American governments forced them to drop this project at the very beginning of the Peace Conference.

In the mind of its supporters, this plan would have enabled France to assure her security by herself. But the Peace Conference had made its decision. Henceforth the security of France could be assured only by collective assistance or by a system of alliances giving France a permanent military superiority over Germany. Now this is what I believed to be the decisive point: French military superiority could not last forever, it could not even last for a long time. Already the United States, then England, were returning to their traditional policy of isolation. Italy, badly hurt by her internal dissension, was breaking away from France. Russia, outlawed by her revolution, could not help making soon an agreement with vanquished Germany. A day would come when peace would be at the mercy of a slight disturbance of the balance of power. Because of the increasing numerical superiority of the German people, the balance would be upset to the disadvantage of France, and there would be another slaughter, more thorough than the last, a

NATIONALISM AND PACIFISM

slaughter which France could not survive. The traditional balance of power system could be upheld in times when wars were not total wars, in times when there were neither universal conscription nor machine guns nor poison gases, nor quick-firing guns, nor bombings from the air. In those days, nations could afford to take the chance of having the balance of their forces disturbed from time to time. But such times were over, and the organization of the international community seemed to me an absolutely vital necessity for the nations of Europe, and most of all for France.

A rudimentary form of international organization existed already. This was the League of Nations, founded by the Treaty of Versailles. The work which remained to be done was plainly outlined: to consolidate this organization, to clarify its principles, to increase the juridical guarantees which would make it the instrument of an equal justice for all, conquerors and conquered alike, to strengthen its legal and moral authority, and finally to provide it with means of coercion which no insurgent could hold in check. It was certainly a difficult undertaking. But would it be easy to go through another European war? The easy thing would be to do nothing, and let things take their course. There remained but two possibilities for

France and the world: the success of the League of Nations and war. As a matter of fact the opponents of the League of Nations were mostly illusionists, who believed that all would go well, provided France had a "strong army" (a little later they would put their confidence in the Maginot Line), cynics, sadists and people who calmly resigned themselves to the catastrophes of the future with the hope that the deluge would not come within their lifetime.

Yes, the consolidation of the League of Nations was a difficult task, and Bergson spoke the truth when he wrote in 1931 that the results obtained had surpassed all that could reasonably have been expected.[8] (It was later on that the decisive blows were dealt.) Among the obstacles to the development of international institutions, none was more effective than the ill-will of an important section of French opinion. It was up to the intellectuals to take seriously a question which concerned the future of their country in such an obviously vital way, and to enlighten public opinion to the best of their abilities.

[8] This remark in *The Two Sources of Morality and Religion* comes from a sound pessimism. Apparently Bergson had understood what tremendous efforts were necessary to have the League of Nations reach a state where it could function with any kind of regularity, and how foolish it would have been to expect only success from it.

At the time I was a young student, the only intellectuals who did anything in favor of the League of Nations were some democrats, without any fighting spirit and rather bourgeois in their way of living and speaking. Most of them were connected with the Liberal or the Socialist party. They were well-intentioned people, at least as sincere as the average run of the intelligentsia, and rather conscientious in their work. Among them were some excellent jurists, men of sane judgment and persons very competent in international relations. Some were not without fervor; but on the whole, their work lacked vigor, doctrinal strength, freshness and determination. Because they had no driving enthusiasm, they never became numerous. They produced serious studies, they never succeeded in launching a myth. As soon as the crisis came, they were swept away by those possessed with a spirit of violence.

It goes without saying that the Communists jeered at the League of Nations, which they depicted as a middle class institution and a hypocritical instrument of international capitalism (theses to be taken up later by a number of noisy anti-Communists). As a matter of fact, the Communist intellectuals were then playing a rather unimportant role. Few educated people could stand the reading of their party papers, filled with base attacks and written in a very bad style.

The political horizon of the French intellectuals was entirely dominated by the lightning success of the *Action Française* group. The importance of the role played by the *Action Française* in the political life of contemporary France can hardly be overrated. This movement started more than forty years ago. A few cultured men had joined together in order to seek, through a fresh approach, the solution of the *French problem*, which none of the traditional groups seemed able to furnish. Soon a leader, Charles Maurras, arose among them. He had the solution: it was the restoration of the hereditary monarchy, and the complete liquidation of the institutions and ideas born of the French Revolution. The restoration of monarchy was certainly not a new idea; what distinguished the royalism of the *Action Française* from the traditional royalist party was the radicalism of its doctrine, the fiery temperament of its supporters, finally their peculiar position in regard to the religious question. Charles Maurras and several of his foremost disciples were atheists or agnostics. Several passages of a strongly anti-Christian tone could be found in the work of Maurras. While the old royalist party appealed mostly to pious aristocrats, former papal Zouaves, and sons of papal Zouaves, the new movement appealed to all, whether believers or unbelievers, who were willing to reject the whole heritage of the French Revolution. Very cleverly, the *Action Française*, claimed to be *the organ of integral nationalism*, thus inviting its readers to consider it self-evident that integral nationalism was identical with its monarchical doctrine. The traditional royalist circles (*doting conservatives*, as Maurras called them), at first gave a cool reception to this group of young intellectuals who spoke with such assurance. Philip of Orléans, the pretender to the French Crown, refused for a time to recognize the members of the *Action Française* as true servants of his cause. Catholics distrusted a movement led by an atheist, and were also afraid that the cause of the Church would again, to the great detriment of apostolic work, appear bound up with the cause of monarchy.

During the war of 1914-1918, the *Action Française* played a brilliant and noisy part; while many of its members distinguished themselves on the battlefield, its daily paper was carrying on relentless campaigns against traitors, defeatists and the faltering. These campaigns no doubt were filled with numberless lies, but the general effect had a fine aspect of patriotic exaltation. About 1922 the *Action Française* had absorbed a good number of its former adversaries. The Duke of Orleans gave it his full support. In the chateaux, traditional strongholds of the royalist party, no paper was read but *L'Action Française*; the French royalist movement had become completely identified with the *Action Française*; veterans of Christian democracy came to it repentantly.

But above all, the *Action Française* had conquered a considerable part of the intellectual world. Parisian students, who in the nineteenth century had been the vanguard of liberal and socialistic democracy, constituted its main force. Among the professors and authors of renown, many recommended the *Action Française* and let themselves be recommended by it. Famous theologians were not afraid to use their sacred science to build up its rather dubious doctrine. This astonishing success was constantly sustained by writers who made the paper *L'Action Française*. The lover of belles-lettres, provided he was not too particular about truth and justice, was assured an hour of bliss every morning providing he subscribed to *L'Action Française*. There was the daily article by Léon Daudet, racy, violent, joyous, full of witty sayings which provoked laughter, and were easily remembered;

there was the daily article of Charles Maurras, sententious, grave, doctrinal, and coldly ruthless; and there was the daily article of Jacques Bainville, who wrote as well as Voltaire. Press reviews, literary surveys, book reviews, all were admirably composed. The strength of the paper was due above all to the systematic mind of its writers. Whatever might be the topics suggested by the daily news, a small number of ideas were repeated indefatigably. The system of the *Action Française* covered all that is talked about: politics, social problems, philosophy, religion, history, literature, medicine, and cooking. Each issue of the paper, or nearly each, comprised an exposition of the system, cleverly summed up in a small number of clichés, always the same, which the reader knew by heart at the end of a month, and repeated with as much pleasure as though he had devised them himself. An habitual reader of *L'Action Française* had an answer for everything, and it never occurred to him to question the validity of what he was taught with such dogmatic assurance and literary talent.

Léon Daudet is such a born novelist that he is the first person not to know where reality ends and fiction begins in his own writings. No paper indulged in calumny, lying, consistent fiction, and insult with more imperturbable regularity than

L'Action Française. The reader swallowed everything with a perfect spirit of discipline. The credulity of the readers of *L'Action Française* was fantastic; it was clear that the constant drilling into their minds of the system's axioms produced in the long run a comfortable inhibition of the power of thinking. Was this credulity entirely free from guilt? This is what became doubtful when the *Action Française*, at the time of its revolt against the Church, directed its slanders against prelates and bishops. Then many of its readers felt a pious indignation; but as long as the *Action Française* simply calumniated Jews, Freemasons, socialists and Christian democrats, they never doubted the veracity of their paper.

Powerful among all the intelligentsia, the *Action Française* exercised at the time we are describing an almost complete dictatorship over Catholic intellectual circles. Whoever came out as a democrat in these circles was doomed to be the object of an ironical and scornful pity; he was looked down upon as a person behind the times, a survivor of another age. In order to appear up to date and to succeed in your career you had to denounce liberal errors with an air of self-satisfied superiority, scoff at liberty, equality and fraternity, joke about progress, look skeptical when human dignity and the rights of conscience were spoken of, affirm authoritatively that every plan for international order was a bloody dream, and sneer at the League of Nations. All of this went on in an atmosphere of impudent arrogance.

The main lines of the international policy of the *Action Française* were extremely simple. The *Action Française* bitterly resented the preservation of German unity by the treaties of 1919. According to it, the preservation of German unity coupled with the dismemberment of the Austro-Hungarian empire, had been engineered by Jews, Freemasons, and Protestants, supported in their shady undertakings by their brethren of the English and American democracies. But since the preservation of German unity was a *fait accompli*, these retrospective considerations had merely a polemical interest. What should be done now? Fight every concession to defeated Germany and every proposal of reconciliation with Germany; proclaim that there were not two Germanies, but only one, and completely dedicated to revenge; oppose relentlessly any attempt to organize international relations juridically; avoid tying up the policy of France with that of England; refuse to disarm; maintain existing alliances and cultivate the friendship of the Latin nations; but above all, destroy, by no matter what means, the Republic and restore the king; once the king had been restored, all problems would be solved.

The king was not restored, but the Republic was destroyed in circumstances known to all. This is what M. Charles Maurras wrote on this subject six months after the defeat of France[9]: ". . . The evening of June 18th, after leaving Paris, we were sadly awaiting another train near Tours; I had then the honor and pleasure of meeting a prophetess, or more exactly a young astrologer well versed in the celestial movements which regulate human affairs and clever in reading our future in the heavens . . .

"This young French girl repeated directly the warning that she had already given me in Paris, several weeks before the German attack in May, through Madame X, her sister. There were not any favorable stars except on one thing: once the disaster and the rout are confirmed, our ideas would be extremely close to being adopted by the public power . . .

"What our reason had always considered as the inevitable outcome of republican anarchy had baffled our imagination, which was not strong enough to represent anything like that, and now the

[9] *Candide*, Jan. 15, 1941.

beautiful star of reactions, a hundred and a thousand times the object of calculations, predictions and even descriptions, had burst like the most unexpected and most fantastic bomb right under our nose and at our feet."

In the first years of the postwar period, the only Catholics who worked resolutely in favor of a Franco-German reconciliation and the League of Nations, were the men of the *Jeune-République*. I collaborated with them for about two years.

The *Jeune-République* represented the left wing of Christian democracy. Its leaders were the veterans of the *Sillon*. A few facts about the *Sillon* must be recalled here.

In the last years of the nineteenth century, a former officer in the Engineers, Marc Sangnier, had founded under this name a youth movement which soon enjoyed an extraordinary influence. It was the time when anti-religious propaganda was raging among the working masses. In public meetings, which were always violent and sometimes bloody, the teaching of atheistic anarchists and socialists was courageously answered by young Sillonists, full of the sacramental life and burning with generosity. The action of the *Sillon* was at once religious, political, and social. Its ideal was

Christian democracy. From the movement sprang a doctrine, and the movement was doomed to perish because of the weakness of the doctrine it had generated. In spite of the very pure faith of its leaders, the *Sillon* let itself unwittingly be invaded by several modernistic errors. In 1910 Pope Pius X issued a letter of condemnation. The Sillonists submitted with an edifying fervor.

The league of the *Jeune-République*, presided over by Marc Sangnier, united a part of the former members of the *Sillon*. It was not, like the *Sillon*, a group devoted principally to religious action. It was a political group whose adherents were for the most part fervent Catholics. Marc Sangnier was the only one among them who was widely known. A man of great kindness and keen intelligence, he had specialized for many years in oratory. All evidence suggested that he read little and never wrote. To know him well you had to see him before an audience of two thousand people, stimulated by the heckling of the Communists, developing the program of the *Jeune-République* in a marvelously constructed speech which sometimes lasted more than two hours without the size of the audience diminishing appreciably. Marc Sangnier was in many respects a man of 1848; he had the emotional ardor of a romanticist and a very romantical disposition to believe that a single idea could be applied successfully to all problems of political and social life. The idea of Marc Sangnier was the democratic idea understood in the most traditional manner. To socialism he opposed industrial democracy; to nationalism, he opposed international democracy organized in a League of Nations which would receive its power, not by a delegation of governments, but by a vote of the peoples. The whole system was permeated with an individualistic psychology which perhaps constituted its weakest point. Marc Sangnier and his friends never missed a chance to assert that nothing good can be done without the inner conversion of souls, and that in particular charity ought to reign in our hearts in order that peace might reign in the world. These ideas would have been entirely true had they been properly balanced by an understanding of the enormous role played in the determination of individual and collective conduct by juridical, economic and technical factors,—in short by sociological factors.

The action of the *Jeune-République* in the first years of the postwar period was devoted entirely to the work of moral education in favor of peace. Political results were slight or nonexistent. Yet there are still today in the world some people who have not forgotten those *International Democratic Congresses* where men of good will, coming from nations separated by chasms of hatred, learned to know each other, and pledged themselves never to hate one another. And some courage was certainly needed to have a German delegation appear in Paris in 1922, and a French delegation in Friburg-in-Brisgau in 1923.

As far as I was concerned, I was happy to give public evidence of my scorn for the anti-German prejudice which at that time possessed the Catholic bourgeoisie. However, there was, in the activities of the *Jeune-République* in favor of peace, something which seemed to me rather disturbing: it was the ambiguity of the term *pacifism*. What is a pacifist? It would be arbitrary to call a pacifist any man who loves peace. On the other hand, two very distinct categories of people can be called pacifists. One category includes those who reject altogether the idea of a just war and declare themselves conscientious objectors; the other includes those who, while affirming that justice sometimes demands recourse to arms, think that preparing for war is not always the best way of assuring peace, and that something ought to be done in order to assure the reign of justice by means less costly and less hazardous than those of war. Between these two categories of people, the difference in attitude is really absolute, since on the decisive question of the just war, one answers *yes*, the other *no*. It is a pity that two absolutely different attitudes should be designated by the same term, and I think that in view of the danger of ambiguity every sane doctrine of peace ought to reject the qualification of pacifist. The leaders of the *Jeune-République* declared themselves pacifists. They were not radical pacifists, for they recognized that war can be just. But for lack of sufficient interest in questions of doctrine, they inclined to act and to think as if the error of the radical pacifists were simply a matter of exaggeration. They collaborated regularly with groups of radical pacifists and did not object to the establishment of a common spirit between the latter and themselves. Such a common spirit could be established only at the expense of truth. I have not forgotten how uneasy I felt in 1924 at a Congress held in London, when I found myself surrounded by Quakers and other non-conformists who formally refused to wage war under any circumstances whatsoever. While a member of a Congress dedicated to pacifist action, I spent my time defending the notion of the just war. I understood then the truism that collaboration is impossible among people who are at variance on some essential point. A year later I quit the *Jeune-République*.

During the last few years before the present war the spirit of absolute pacifism developed enormously in democratic countries; it penetrated certain Catholic circles where it became customary to evade the doctrine of the Church on the just war by arguing that there can not be a just war under the conditions of modern warfare. In most cases this argument is sheer hypocrisy, for those who refuse to recognize the idea of the just war in the armed resistance to the most obviously abominable tyrannies, ordinarily do not hesitate to proclaim the justice of certain slaughters which please their secret passions. Hypocritical or sincere, Catholic or not, the spirit of absolute pacifism became, consciously or otherwise, the ally of treachery and cowardice. When the students of Oxford declared that they did not wish to fight for their king and their country, Hitler knew he did not have to curb his ambition.[10]

We were not absolute pacifists, but we fell into another error, an error not of doctrine, but of historical and political judgment. In the first postwar

[10] It is needless to recall that these errors of a day did not prevent the Oxford students from defending their country and their king with magnificent courage.

years, we used to stress the fact that there were two Germanies: the militaristic Germany which sought revenge, and the democratic Germany (partly Catholic and partly Socialist) which wanted peace and could not help but want peace. Franco-German rapprochement and Franco-German collaboration seemed to us possible and extremely desirable because, as we used to say, democratic Germany was in power. If we had been logical and true to our initial position, we should have rejected absolutely every policy of rapprochement, every policy of concession, and we should have demanded a policy of uncompromising resistance immediately after the defeat of democratic Germany. We should have demanded the same policy of uncompromising resistance toward Italian Fascism. We did not have enough fortitude to do this. We, who understood that the consolidation of democratic Germany was the most indispensable condition for peace in Europe, failed to see, for lack of fortitude, that the era of peaceful relations had come to an end the day Hitler became Chancellor of the Reich. We did not have enough will-power to understand that the first thing to do was to rid Europe of Nazism and of Fascism. We did not have enough will-power to realize (soon enough) that the same will for peace which required an agreement with democratic Germany, demanded a rupture with Nazi Germany. We had rightly advocated a conciliatory attitude toward democratic Germany; others actually adopted an attitude of conciliation and endless concessions toward Nazi Germany. We failed to realize that they were doing precisely the contrary of what we had wanted to do. Deceived by certain superficial similarities and hampered in our work by the weakness of our characters, we did not understand soon enough what a difference there was between the consolidation of the forces of peace we had wanted, and the diabolical contribution to the triumph of the forces of destruction that the *policy of appeasement* was to be.

IV

Politics and Religion

The disaster of France could not help being exploited all over the world by certain commentators of whom the Book of Job gives a familiar portrait; they are bold interpreters of the designs of Providence, and can recognize in the suffering of their neighbor the well-deserved punishment of his impiety. They consider themselves secure against any similar punishment, and their air of smug complacency indicates that all will go well for those who will simply follow their advice.

A bit of history suffices to unmask these wise men and to restore to its rights the mystery of the ways of Providence. The religious history of contemporary France gives the overwhelming impression of a divine mystery revealing itself amidst the human turmoil. Then there is no longer any place for pharisaic rhetoric, but only for adoration, repentance and hope.

On the eve of the first World War, France was already giving signs of a return to the Faith. However, her temporal life was dominated by legislation opposed in many respects to the rights of God and the Church. Let us recall briefly the main provisions of the famous *laic laws*.

Completely separated from the Church, the State professed religious neutrality and considered religion a private affair. The modest compensation guaranteed to the clergy by Napoleon's Concordat had been suppressed: a great deal of Church property had been seized without the slightest semblance of justice. Many religious orders had been expelled and all were forbidden to teach. Public schools and most hospitals formerly run by religious orders had been given to lay persons. Secondary public schools were allowed to retain their chaplains, but no priest could exercise his ministry in primary public schools. Of all these provisions the most productive of evil were those concerning hospitals and schools. Every patient in a hospital had the right to ask for a priest, but frequently there was nobody who dared warn him that death was near. Countless men died without the sacraments as a result of a law which gave them complete freedom to receive the sacraments if they so wished. Many grade school teachers were militant free-thinkers. Even if all of them had thoroughly respected religious beliefs, as the law required them to do, countless children would nonetheless have grown up without the Faith for lack of hearing anything about religion in their daily school training. The freedom of teaching was legally guaranteed, but Catholic schools had been deprived of their best teachers by the suppression of teaching orders. Moreover, lack of money made it very difficult for them to withstand the competition of the public schools.

Had we to account for the genesis of this anti-Christian legislation, we should have to go a long way back in history, and take into consideration a multitude of factors. Let us rather mention that at the time these laic laws were passed, anti-clerical feeling, far from being limited to certain political groups, was widespread among the masses. But the sufferings of the war awakened in many souls a nostalgia for God. The revival of the religious spirit, already noticeable for some years in educated circles, grew more rapidly during the years of trial.

God draws good from evil, and the conscription of priests, an iniquitous concession to popular anti-clericalism, helped to diminish the anti-clerical prejudices of the French people. Many poor fellows who had never known priests except through sinister legends learned in the companionship of military life what a man of God is.

The election of 1919 sent to Parliament a proportion of practicing Catholics much larger than that of the preceding legislatures and much larger than the proportion of practicing Catholics in the nation as a whole. The embassy at the Vatican was reestablished; the feast of St. Joan of Arc became a national feast of the Republic. These were, in the opinion of all, signs of a new spirit. The banished religious orders began to return. However, none of the laic laws was modified. Although some of them were less and less enforced, the idea prevailed among unbelieving politicians that it was a good precaution to keep all of them in reserve against any possible counter-offensive of clericalism. On the other hand, most Catholic politicians seem to admit that an attempt at the formal revision of the laic laws would be premature and that it was better to wait until they had unquestionably become obsolete.

The Chamber of 1919 represented a break in the

progress of the Liberal and Socialist parties. Rightly or wrongly, its tendencies were believed to represent a phase of reaction in the general movement of democracy in France. Its work did not satisfy anybody. This Chamber had been elected in a great outburst of patriotic fervor, with the mandate of assuring the reparation of the great devastation suffered by France, and of consolidating peace. The reconstruction of the regions ravaged by the war had been pursued with great efficiency, but the condition of the national finances was very bad. The occupation of the Ruhr District in 1923 had exasperated the resentment of the Germans and caused strong dissatisfaction in England. Many people had understood that a change in foreign policy was necessary, that the Ruhr should be evacuated, that the problem of reparations should be given a psychologically tolerable form, and that collaboration with England should be resumed. The Leftist parties were to exploit this situation thoroughly.

The most important of these parties were the Liberal and Socialist parties. Because of the provisions of the electoral system they could not win a major success unless they formed a coalition. There were serious divergencies between the two parties and their union was difficult to achieve. Although the Socialist party had been rid of its most violent elements by the formation of the Communist party, it still remained a revolutionary party; it still pretended to be a class party and the parliamentary representative of the proletariat; it still remained firmly attached to the principle of class struggle. In foreign policy, it opposed systematically every expression, reasonable or not, of French nationalism, and its propaganda resounded with rather vague slogans, rightly considered as disturbing by those who did not share the Socialist faith: *the union of the workingmen will bring peace to the world, the suppression of capitalism will mean the end of wars*, etc. In financial matters, the Socialists demanded certain reforms extremely repugnant to the property owning class (tax on capital).

The idea of class struggle was foreign to the Liberal party. Its chief idea was the democratic notion of people, not the socialist notion of proletariat. It was an essentially bourgeois party, a party of property owners; it was the parliamentary representative of the anti-clerical section both of the bourgeoisie and of the rural world. In financial policy, it was more inclined than the Rightist groups to favor state-socialistic solutions, but it took great care not to displease the middle classes, so firmly attached to their property. It was easy to arouse against it the resentment of the working class for Liberal governments had, more than once, employed armed force to break up strikes. In international matters the Liberal party was favorable to a policy of understanding with German democracy and of cordial cooperation with Great Britain. But the *internationalistic* spirit of socialism was uncongenial to it, and it distrusted the uncautious measures advocated by the Socialists as regards disarmament.

Since union was necessary, despite so many divergencies, the two parties had to emphasize all they had in common. Now, the tenet the two parties had most unquestionably in common was anti-clericalism. The electoral campaign of 1924 was violently anti-clerical. It resulted in an overwhelming victory for the Leftist Coalition (*Cartel des Gauches*). Once more, anti-clericalism had been successfully employed as a plank in an electoral contest.

Edouard Herriot, leader of the Liberal party, was designated by the election for the Presidency of the Council. After him, the man in the political limelight was Léon Blum, leader of the Socialist party. One of the first gestures of Herriot was the publication of a letter to Blum containing the program of the new government. This program included the strict enforcement of the laws concerning religious congregations, the suppression of the embassy at the Vatican, and the introduction of the laic laws in Alsace-Lorraine.

When the French troops marched into Alsace at the beginning of the war, the commander-in-chief, General Joffre, had solemnly promised the population that their religious customs would be respected. It was thoroughly realized in France that the Alsacians would not accept the religious legislation established by the Third Republic. The promises of Joffre had been confirmed after the Armistice. On the ground of the juridical fact that the people of Alsace-Lorraine, separated from France by the treaty of Frankfurt, were not represented in Parliament at the time the laic laws were passed, it was decided that the Concordat was still valid in Alsace-Lorraine and that the public schools would remain denominational, with courses of religion required. This compromise had functioned for four years, not without difficulties, but on the whole in a rather satisfactory manner.

The declarations of the Herriot government provoked a great deal of indignation in Alsace and throughout France. Unions of resistance organized everywhere. Press and poster campaigns, big demonstrations, expressed an unshakable resolution. The anti-clerical project died down; two years later, it was forgotten. The religious communities which were still abroad returned one after another. Schools conducted by religious orders increased in number and became less and less particular about hiding their identity. In the last years of the Third Republic the laws concerning the congregations had fallen completely into disuse. The Vichy government, in declaring them abolished, did nothing more than proclaim the just recognition of a *fait accompli*.

The anti-clerical adventure of the Leftist Coalition suggests some conclusions which can be summarized in the following terms: 1) In 1924 it was still possible to utilize anti-clericalism successfully in an electoral platform. 2) Unlike what happened twenty years earlier, the French Catholics had shown themselves capable of victorious resistance. 3) The main weapon of this resistance had been the appeal to public opinion. It had very soon become clear that public opinion would not support a new persecution of religious orders.

The crisis provoked by the anti-religious program of the Leftist Coalition had hardly died down when another politico-religious crisis broke out. In the summer of 1926 Cardinal Andrieu, Archbishop of Bordeaux, published a letter exhorting the young people of his diocese to withdraw from the organizations of the *Action Française*. The document was extremely violent. Was it entirely just? The least that can be said is that it gave evidence of hasty composition. A little later, newspapers published a short letter in which the Holy Father gave his approbation to Cardinal Andrieu. It was explicitly declared that the question of the political regime was not at stake; French Catholics had every right to campaign for the restoration of the monarchy, if they thought it wise, but they were strongly urged not to adhere to the *Action Française*.

We have shown in an earlier chapter the extent of the influence won by the *Action Française* in the Catholic world. The number of persons who believed that the rechristianization of France could only be brought about by a political victory of the *Action Française* had constantly increased in the course of the preceding years. The intervention of the Pope could not help producing a dreadful conflict in many consciences.

For some time the significance of this intervention appeared uncertain. Did the Pope mean that Catholics should leave the *Action Française* movement and cease to read its paper? These doubts were soon cleared up. The *Action Française* openly revolted against the supreme authority. The paper was put on the Index. Joining and supporting the movement were forbidden under the most severe canonical penalties. Many believed that the *Action Française* could not survive so great a crisis. Yet it did survive. The ban was lifted thirteen years later, in 1939, by His Holiness Pope Pius XII, after the *Action Française* had published a letter of retraction.

The consequences of the condemnation of the *Action Française* were extremely significant. Among the Catholics who had adhered to the movement, there were three main types of reaction.

Some refused openly to submit, claiming that the condemnation directed against them was an abuse of authority and could not bind in conscience. According to them, this condemnation was only the result of political intrigues in which the hand of Germany, that of the Freemasons, etc., could be recognized. And many stories went on, some of them very grossly and gratuitously insulting to the Pope, his advisors and representatives. It is impossible to make any conjecture about the number of these Catholics who preferred to live in revolt against the Church for thirteen years rather than give up their political allegiance. All evidence suggests that they were many. What about the religious life of these rebels? Some lived without the sacraments for thirteen years, while others continued to frequent the sacraments they were forbidden to receive.

These rebels had little direct influence on the French Catholic world as a whole. But very close to them was another category of people, ready to act as go-betweens for the *Action Française*. They were those who practiced a literal submission and nothing more. They abstained from anything which would obviously have forbidden them absolution, but their abstention went no further. They no longer read *L'Action Française*, they did not renew their membership in the *Action Française* movement, they no longer contributed their savings for its maintenance. But they read the papers which most resembled *L'Action Française* and kept its spirit alive within themselves. In Paris as well as in the provinces, a number of papers devoted themselves to this ambiguous work: providing the former readers of *L'Action Française* the ideological and emotional diet they needed, without, however, preventing them from receiving absolution. This farce was played with masterly cleverness. To be deprived of reading *L'Action Française* became tolerable, since no letter from the Holy Father forbade the reading of *Candide*, edited by Jacques

Bainville and in which Léon Daudet wrote regularly; *Gringoire* in which pornography was harmoniously combined with polemics of an unheard of vileness; *Je Suis Partout* where names made famous by *L'Action Française* were recognized, and which only later revealed its connections with the Nazis; and all those "pious" local papers, the self-appointed defenders of religion against liberal and socialist sheets, which contained daily criticisms that coincided so exactly with those of *L'Action Française*! The spirit of *L'Action Française* made enormous progress during the thirteen years of its condemnation, and this progress was not only the work of unbelievers and refractory Catholics; it was in large part the work of Catholics who practiced submission to the letter of the condemnation.

Nevertheless, the action of the Church, carried on in the sometimes disconcerting mystery of human contingencies, bore admirable fruit. Besides the rebels and those who submitted only to the letter, there were those who submitted completely and who, as a reward for their submission, received the grace of a marvelous interior purification. I knew several of them. Before the Holy Father's intervention, they had never suspected that there might be anything pernicious in *L'Action Française*. With the naïveté of novices, they had swallowed every morning for some years the fantastic stories, calumnies and fallacious arguments with which their newspaper was accustomed to feed its readers. The papal censures had at first seemed incomprehensible to them, and as long as their significance had remained uncertain, they had hesitated. But, when the condemnation bound them to choose between revolt and obedience, they responded with a great act of filial obedience, pronounced in the purifying awe of a complete darkness. It was said that the condemnation of the *Action Française* marked the end of French anti-clericalism; that is plausible, but what is certain is that it liberated the *mystical energy* which was to make the last years of the Third Republic a great epoch in the religious history of France. Henceforth, the way was open to those who aspired to an entirely pure religious life, at last cleared of all the poisonous by-products that some temporal groups, in their selfishness and their stupidity, employ to corrupt religious consciences.

An example will show precisely the kind of secret corruption we have in mind. Some years ago, just after the death of Dreyfus, a Catholic review published a short article in which you might have read something like this: "Now that the innocence of Dreyfus has been definitely established, the papers which once campaigned against him would do well to retract their error." Following the publication of this article, the editor of the review had the honor of being summoned by a high Catholic personality.

"So, Reverend Father, you praise traitors?" The Reverend Father replied that his review had not praised treachery, but had simply recalled that the act of treason first attributed to a certain officer, Captain Dreyfus, had really been committed by another officer, Captain Esterhazy. That was all. Then this high Catholic personality exclaimed: "Well! What would my family say if they heard you say that Dreyfus was not a traitor!" (It was a family of rich bankers.) This high Catholic personality believed *sincerely* in the guilt of Dreyfus. The supreme service rendered to a great number of souls by the condemnation of the *Action Française* was to teach them to go beyond that sort of sincerity. When faced by a question of justice and truth, there are people who wonder what their family will think if the facts fail to support the version which flatters most the interests, hatreds and prejudices of the family. Others try to know the truth and to declare themselves according to the demands of justice, without bothering about how it will affect the fortunes of their family.

The readers of *L'Action Française* had the habit

of thinking about any problem under discussion what *L'Action Française* thought about it. Did they submit to the condemnation? Those who did proved willing—at the cost of a descent into the darkness—to think no longer like *L'Action Française* on a point it judged the most important of all. The freedom-giving break had been so violent and so complete that henceforth no servitude could ever seduce them. And thus we had the privilege of witnessing the growth of a few souls free from everything except from Christ. The radiant influence of these souls was to be extraordinary.

Henceforth it would be easier to make appeals for foreign missions without falling back upon the traditional argument so harmful to apostolic action: missionaries are the best agents of French influence abroad. Henceforth it would be easier to make appeals for Catholic education without giving first place to the consideration that the Catholic school, by keeping the future workingmen away from socialism, contributes to the tranquillity of bourgeois families. Henceforth it would be easier to promote Catholic labor unions without bothering about the opinions of some Catholic employers who spoke of "our adversaries" in referring to Catholic trade unionists. Henceforth it would be easier to teach the Christian sense of poverty without attaching too much importance to its possible conflicts with the middle class sense of security. Henceforth the struggle for the freedom of religious orders would no longer look like an attempt in favor of a spiritual police dangerous to republican institutions. Henceforth whenever the forces of deception and iniquity attempted to subdue the Catholic world, some respected and powerful Catholic voices would be raised in favor of truth and justice.

During the summer of 1937 a great Frenchman and one of the noblest Christians I have ever been privileged to meet, told me how impressed he was by some new trends in the collective conscience of French Catholics. "A crisis like the Dreyfus case," he said, "would not be possible to-day." It is very striking that one cannot write on the history of contemporary France without frequently referring to this epoch-making affair. It was a juridical crisis, a national crisis, a social and an ideological crisis; the Dreyfus case was also a religious crisis, since nearly all French Catholics, blinded by the passions of the groups with which they had foolishly cast their lot, supported the version of Captain Dreyfus' guilt. Now, it was a fact that Captain Dreyfus was innocent and that the treason had been committed by another Captain, named Esterhazy. But Dreyfus was a Jew,

Esterhazy was not; consequently the guilty one had to be Dreyfus. The cause of Dreyfus was defended by the Republican party, numerous Freemasons and the Socialist party; consequently the guilty one had to be Dreyfus. Among the partisans of Dreyfus there were many enemies of the Church, of the army and of the political order; consequently the guilty one had to be Dreyfus. The real facts mattered little. What mattered was the triumph of a party—the anti-Dreyfus party. And in order that this party should triumph, the guilty one had to be Dreyfus. With very few exceptions, French Catholics committed themselves unreservedly in the anti-Dreyfus campaign and against justice. It was justice that triumphed. Dreyfus was vindicated. But this triumph of justice involved dishonor for those who had fought justice. No honest historian contests the fact that the persecution of the Catholics at the beginning of the century was determined in large measure by the attitude of the Catholics during the Dreyfus case.

Thus a great Frenchman told me in 1937 that if a new Dreyfus case came up it would not be again possible to produce the devastating scandal of the Catholic world standing to a man, or nearly so, in favor of a judicial error. We had indeed noticed, in the course of the preceding years, that in spite of the pressure exercised by political cliques, it had not been possible to marshal the French Catholics in favor of dubious or infamous causes. Whenever unanimity seemed assured, a handful of men raised their voice to assert the truth. How extensive a support they had in the masses, was evidenced by the innumerable testimonies which came to them from humble souls full of gratitude toward those whose independent attitude had relieved their conscience. Here are a few examples.

In 1934, following the Stavisky scandal and the riots of February 6th, the situation seemed ripe for the establishment of Fascism in France. It would have been very nice to have French Catholics favor unanimously the *coup d'état* contemplated against democratic liberties. One could believe that the unanimity of the Catholics would be easily achieved, for it was a perfect occasion to fight the Freemasons as at the time of the Dreyfus case. But some Catholics had understood that the pleasure of fighting Freemasons ought not to prevail over the common good of the country. A manifesto entitled *For the Common Good*, signed by fifty-two Catholic writers, sufficed to make known that Christian France would not permit her cause to be identified with that of Fascism. In 1935 the Italian government attacked Ethiopia in defiance of pledged faith; this was a typical example of an unjust war. Propaganda soon raged, the mobilization of the Catholics began (throughout the world), Catholic papers (with few exceptions) rallied to the side of force. A manifesto *For Justice and Peace*, published by a group of Catholic writers, made such an impression that honest Christians no longer felt isolated and were given a new courage to carry on their tasks. In 1936, the Minister of the Interior, Roger Salengro, was the object of a slander campaign of unheard of violence. He was accused of having voluntarily surrendered to the enemy during the war. The fact was never proved. On the other hand, it was known that Salengro had shown courageous conduct during his captivity in Germany. As a political figure, Salengro deserved the most severe criticism; he was a socialist who had been prominent in the anti-clerical battles of the past. But so far as his military honor was concerned, the only certain thing was that as a prisoner of war he had risked being shot by organizing a strike in a German factory.

The campaign against the honor of the Minister was led by *Gringoire*, the most abject of the Rightist papers. The pornographic character of this paper should have prevented it from reaching Catholic circles. But political passion can occasionally facilitate the distribution of pornographic products, just as in other circumstances it is pornography which facilitates the distribution of political products. The Rightist papers almost unanimously echoed this campaign of *Gringoire*, and when the Chamber of Deputies passed a vote of censure on this campaign, the Rightist groups, to which most of the Catholic politicians belonged, refused to take part in this act of simple decency.

One morning Salengro was found dead in his kitchen, the gas jet open. On the table, the desperate man had left a note saying that, broken down by slander, he wanted to join his wife who had died some years before. (She too had been a victim of a campaign of slander; she was accused of having bestowed her favors on German soldiers during the war, but this time the accusation came from Communists.) That day, one of my friends, a young professor, was giving a class in a Catholic girls school. At the end of the class he found the head of the school waiting for him. She was beaming. "Have you heard the news? Salengro has committed suicide. His suicide is a confession of guilt." The young teacher answered that before coming to any conclusion on the meaning of the suicide, it would be better to await further information. The shrew replied: "It is all clear. *Grin-*

goire was just about to publish in its next issue a devastating document, the testimony of the German non-commissioned officer to whom Salengro surrendered." Then the young teacher remarked that this was pushing absurdity too far; that a non-commissioned officer, while taking a prisoner, would hardly think of fixing in his mind the details of the incident so as to be able to reproduce them twenty years later when his prisoner had become a Minister. The girls of the school listened to the conversation; they also rejoiced at the idea that the suicide was a confession, and felt indignant that their teacher should doubt a truth so indispensable to the emotional life of their families as the desertion of Salengro.

This little story illustrates nicely the character of the forces which were relentlessly harrassing the French Catholics; their work of corruption did not even spare the souls of children. We had to deal with moral gangsters who did not hesitate to steal the souls of little girls in schools dedicated to the Blessed Mother. Those people, it is easy to understand, would have liked to be left alone in their work. But two days later the local papers published a letter from the Bishop of the diocese, severely rebuking the slander and invoking divine mercy on the soul of the suicide. A manifesto *In Defence of Honor* was likewise published, in which the reader could recognize many names already seen in the manifestoes *For the Common Good* and *For Justice and Peace*.

Some months later, Nazi aviators held a final rehearsal of the tactics of mass slaughter by bombing and machine gunning that they employed so successfully later at Warsaw and Rotterdam. The spot chosen for this try-out was a small Catholic city, the holy city of a province known throughout the world as a center of religious fervor. It might have been thought that this event would embarrass those who had assumed the task of winning the complicity of the Catholic world for the greater crimes still in the preparatory stage. They were not at all embarrassed. They were familiar with the maxim of *Mein Kampf* that the greater the lie the better its chances of success, for the average man, who is accustomed to tell small lies, but not great ones, suspects the lie when it is small, but cannot suspect it when it is colossal. It was easy to declare that the holy city had not been attacked by Nazi aviators, but destroyed by its own defenders. They rushed to the scene an old member of the French Academy, M. Claude Farrère. He was a novelist appreciated by the conservative burgeoisie. Because he had been an officer in his youth, M. Farrère could pass himself off as a military expert. His testimony was formal: there had been no attack from the air, but systematic destruction by those who were holding the ground. In the face of the testimony of M. Claude Farrère, the Catholics were requested to discount as null and void the unanimous testimony of the local clergy who had seen the airplanes fly over the city and drop their bombs, who had seen the population flee, then lie flat on the ground under the fire of machine guns. M. Farrère was the man who had written, at the time of the bombing of Shanghai by the Japanese, this unforgettable statement: "After all, T. N. T. was not invented for laboratory experiments." Those who had published *For the Common Good*, *For Justice and Peace*, and *In Defence of Honor*, published one more manifesto, a humble expression of truth and love dedicated to the body-littered remnants of the destroyed city.

These are only poor examples to illustrate the activity of a spirit. This spirit of truth, justice and honor, which occasionally did not refuse to publish manifestoes, produced its most important achievements in the silent work of daily apostolate. Where are they now, these valiant companions, students, workers, teachers, business men, priests and religious, who established everywhere on the soil of France centers of Christian regeneration? Unbelievers came to them, knowing that they were free, recognizing in them the holy freedom of the children of God. Old obstacles to apostolic action, walls of prejudices, were falling one after another. The revolutionary worker, the rationalist intellectual, realized more and more clearly that there were no traps to fear, but only great blessings to expect from those joyous souls inspired not by the "pious" newspapers, but by the living sources of the supernatural life: the teaching of the Church, Catholic discipline, the sacraments, the liturgy, prayer. The movement of return to the Catholic faith, noticeable for a generation in the intellectual world, was reaching the masses in such a way that Christian hearts were throbbing with hope.

"May you be given ten years to work," Maritain told a group of young Catholics in 1938, "and great things will flourish on this earth which now seems desolate."[11]

But the international Nazis did not wish to give the French Catholic youth ten years to work. On the other hand, they could not succeed in their projects without winning the sympathy, or at least the apathy, of Catholics all over the world. Thus

---

[11] *Questions de conscience*, Desclée De Brouwer, Paris, 1939, p. 271.

you can easily understand why and in the service of whom, a campaign of calumnies, so uniform and persevering that it must have been unified somewhere, was launched against Christian France. At the very moment when signs of a magnificent revival of faith and charity were becoming unmistakable in the most varied phases of French life, the rumor spread throughout the world that France was a country completely dominated by atheism, where Catholics themselves had become half Bolshevik. Catholics of the whole world were invited to conclude that there was no reason to move a finger or say a prayer to help save France from Nazi conquest.

V

The Twilight of the Myths

The occupation of the Ruhr district by the French army (1923) had strained to the breaking-point, as we have already mentioned, the tension of Franco-German relations; it had also caused bitter resentment in England. The victory of the Leftist coalition (May, 1924) had been determined partly by the general feeling that the time had come to substitute a democratic policy of international collaboration for the strong arm policy of which the occupation of the Ruhr and the "passive resistance" of the Germans were symbols. In England, the Labor party had just come into power. It was up to the French and the British democracies to establish peaceful relations with the German Republic.

No amount of good will could nullify the enormous difficulties standing in the way of a normal state of affairs in international life. These difficulties were, for the most part, the sheer result of the immense destruction wrought during four years of war. At least, a sincere attempt was made to open an era of peaceful relations. And this attempt did not fail entirely. Between the two world wars there was but one period when Europe was permitted to enjoy a feeling of peace. This period opened in 1924, thanks to the new direction given to European politics by the Liberal government of France and by the Labor government of England.

The Ruhr was evacuated; the problem of reparations was given a less irritating form. Germany came out of the isolation forced upon her; she would soon be admitted into the League of Nations. The reconciliation of the French and German peoples was no longer an hypothesis skeptically dismissed. From then on, it was an object of hope. A year later, the Treaty of Locarno (1925) could be considered as a decisive step toward the establishment of true peace. By this document, France, Germany, Great Britain, Belgium and Italy guaranteed the boundaries established by the Treaty of Versailles between Germany and her neighbors to the West. This implied on Germany's part the definitive renunciation of any claim to Alsace; it implied, on the part of France, that no such performance as the occupation of the Ruhr would ever take place again, and that no other attempt would be made to detach the Rhineland from Germany. The regions still occupied by French troops would be evacuated sooner than the Treaty of Versailles provided for; in return, the German government pledged itself never to build fortifications nor to keep troops in the Rhineland.

The Treaty of Locarno offered the French nationalists a new occasion to display their irony. It was to be violated with impunity ten years later, but the other treaties were also to be brushed aside in the great conflict between the fanatic dynamism of the dictatorships and the irresolution of the democratic countries. Significantly enough, the day the spirit of Locarno—a spirit of cooperation and of reciprocal guaranties—ceased to exist, peace disappeared from Europe.

The short years of appeasement that followed the Treaty of Locarno were years of economic prosperity. Capital flowed into Germany; in France the conjuncture was so favorable that millions of foreign laborers found work there. Owing to the general satisfaction resulting from the easing of economic relations, the preachers of hatred saw their influence decrease, and time was healing many wounds. The French thought less about the devastations suffered during the war; the Germans thought less about the sufferings caused by the blockade, and their helpless rage during the occupation of the Ruhr. Moral disarmament was progressing rapidly. Let us note in particular, that the idea of a supra-national Catholic brotherhood, up to then rather powerless outside of limited circles, developed rapidly both among French and German Catholics.

But all of these happy results, on which great hopes were based, were soon to be jeopardized by a world catastrophe: the economic depression. I spent a year (1929-1930) in Germany when the spirit of Locarno was in its last phase. The region I lived in was a Catholic province in the east. There, at this time, and in the circles (almost exclusively Catholic) that I frequented, a Frenchman was always cordially received. He was the object of a friendly curiosity. In many instances, I observed among my hosts the feeling that all these hatreds and misunderstandings should be done away with, that the French and the German would like each other more if they only knew each other better, that the moment had come to achieve the fruitful collaboration of two great peoples, who, until then,

THE TWILIGHT OF THE MYTHS

had known only how to kill each other. Besides these favorable attitudes regarding the French, I observed in Germany, in the same circles, the growing power of some very disconcerting dispositions. The most striking of all was the hatred of the Pole. A hatred the more ruthless since it was accompanied by contempt. The Frenchman and the German can hate one another, they will never despise one another. Most of the Germans I knew, Prussians or not, Catholics or not, hated the Pole and contemned him. The boundary line of Germany in the East, as it was established by the Treaty of Versailles involved fewer injustices than many amateurs, perfectly ignorant of the ethnic map of Europe, are accustomed to think. Its great mistake was to have created an unbearable psychological situation. The reasonable German accepted without reluctance that Alsace be French. But to accept the existence of a Polish corridor leading to Danzig, the German needed a degree of reasonableness of which few people were capable. And this in spite of the unquestioned fact that the population of the Corridor was by a large majority Polish.

On the other hand, the republican regime founded by the Weimar constitution gave signs of rapid deterioration. A fatal provision of this constitution, the establishment of proportional representation, had resulted in a confusing multiplicity of parties, a weak administration and constant political agitation. Endless quarrels and compromises, that satisfied no one, were creating a growing feeling of impatience. To do away with a constitutional disorder, many people, without thinking too much about what they were doing, would deliver themselves, body and soul, to the first force that would prove capable of making any kind of unity triumph in a nation exhausted by dissension.

All this, and other alarming factors, assumed a singular gravity because of the great fact that dominated everything: the depression. While all memories were still haunted by bewildering recollections of the period of inflation, a present catastrophe filled souls with an ever-increasing horror. One after another, the various categories of workers were thrown out of work, and owing to despair, there would soon be in Germany a mass of several million men resigned to everything, ready for anything. Poverty generally causes the spread of socialism, but, in this particular case, it was exceedingly easy to attribute the misery of the people to the misfortunes of the nation: the defeat, the military occupation, the reparations, the loss of territory. A handful of men had found the formula that would integrate all passions: this formula was the combination of the nationalistic and the socialistic passions. When I left Germany in July, 1930, the National Socialist party of Hitler was still only a noisy minority. It inspired fear, and, owing to the working of proportional representation, its Parliamentary group increased at each election. But very few persons outside of the party itself would ever have thought it possible that in the very near future, Imperial Germany and Republican Germany would capitulate solemnly into the hands of Hitler.

It is well known that the depression was less violent in France than in many other countries. It was felt later in France than in the United States and Germany; it began and developed surreptitiously; it was not at first marked with dramatic shocks. The dismissal of many foreign laborers hid for a while the growth of unemployment. Part-time unemployment prevented the statistics of total unemployment from assuming at once alarming proportions. Widespread anxiety developed slowly; a more and more painful misery settled gradually among the masses. The laboring classes gave evidence of a long-suffering patience. For fear of being thrown into the hell of unemployment, the workers consented almost in silence to incredibly low salaries. On the whole, it is not certain that the effects of the depression were less profound in France than in certain countries where it provoked more brutal and more sensational reactions. The essential result, the establishment of confusion and despair, was brought about just as unmistakably in France as in Germany.

The chief characteristic of the psychology of the French people during these depression years was the barrenness of sociological and political imagination. The various parties and groups were mulling over their traditional solutions, but none of these solutions inspired the slightest movement of creative enthusiasm. Throughout the nineteenth century each great wave of public suffering had given rise to, or reinforced, various utopias and myths; these myths and these utopias, however mixed they may have been with error, had been useful as sources of energy; they had protected countless souls, and often very great ones, against the temptations of selfishness and of despair; by stimulating the social action of those who believed in them, they had favored the selection of a ruling elite and helped to push new men into the foreground. The years of the depression in France were marked by the *twilight of the myths*. Communism inspired a general aversion. The Socialist party, whose position had been wavering since the

Russian Revolution, was aging rapidly. The most active of its new men broke away from it, formed suspicious organizations and unexpected alliances. (They are today the best supporters of Hitler in France.) The Liberal party, with the exception of a few intriguers, had become simply a gathering of old gentlemen. They were so devoid of faith that soon they would no longer even have the strength to be anti-clericals. The moderate and reactionary parties showed complete confusion. Many persons among them were favorable to Fascism but did not dare declare their sympathies, nor express them in consistent rules of action. The French Parliament, whose manners had never been very edifying, tended to become a mere club of politicians ready to follow any policy, because no one knew which was the good policy, because no one any longer dared to assert that the policy he preferred was the one that should actually prevail. There was a great temptation to reap the highest personal advantages from a situation in which no one understood anything. When you no longer know what to do for the commonweal, the only thing you can do, unless you are willing to resign, is to look out for your own personal interests.

In the nation, leagues of civic action were growing in number. The rapid development of some of them evidenced the general discontent. What were these leagues driving at? They avoided disclosing it frankly, perhaps they themselves did not know accurately. Sometimes, they even hid their political character. They used a great number of high-sounding and equivocal words. All of them tended more or less definitely towards Fascism, but they were careful not to say it. It was generally taken for granted that the Fascist regime would not suit the temperament of the French people. In reality, every Fascist regime presupposes one leader, one party, one ideology. Now there were several leaders who detested each other cordially, and none of them succeeded in giving himself the appearance of a great political character. There were as many parties as there were leaders, and there was no ideology at all.

Owing to the lack of creative imagination, visions of destruction haunted without restraint the mind of the public; no positive belief arose to hold them in check. These visions were condensed into two words: *revolution, war*. What was the relationship between them? Some said: revolution *or* war, but most people were under the impression that one calamity would not come without the other, and that both were approaching hesitating France with the fatality of cosmic forces. Leagues and parties proclaimed their determination to prevent revolution and war; in fact it was about the only justification they could give for their existence. But who does not see the consequences of this attitude which was merely one of opposition? The lot of the leagues and parties was bound up with the threat of the very dangers that the leagues and parties allegedly wanted to remove. Thus the two spectres of war and of revolution grew, and covered the nation with a shadow of horror able to provoke all kinds of panic.

This was the situation of the French nation when Hitler was appointed Chancellor of the Reich (January, 1933). It seems to me today that the reaction of the French was predominantly fatalistic. The event was not unexpected. In France, as in Germany, many fools consoled themselves by declaring that a gang of adventurers so devoid of political wisdom would not last long under the test of power. In any case, the military danger was only remote, France would have time to complete her Maginot Line, and the problems of domestic policy retained their primordial importance. This was not all. If the coming to power of Hitler could not help making the visions of war more real and terrifying, it had rather a pacifying effect so far as the fear of revolution was concerned. For some time the French had understood that Germany could not stand for long the condition of violent dissensions and of political instability that characterized the last years of the Weimar Republic. They knew that a change was inevitable. They had feared the worst, and was not the coming into power of the Communist party the worst? Germany had chosen; she had not chosen the worst. There was, therefore, no cause for serious alarm.

And so the legend of Hitler, the conqueror of Communism, won a first victory over the French as early as the first months of 1933. The tanks were to pass seven years later through the breach then opened in the national conscience of France. It was as yet much too soon to praise Hitler and Nazism publicly in France. But the time was admirably chosen to launch a campaign of insinuations whose psychological effect would be considerable. Was this campaign deliberately planned? I rather believe that it was the spontaneous work of party spirit, dragging in tow ignorance and stupidity. It is only later that treachery would come into action.

One of the first acts of the Nazis in power was to set fire to the Reichstag and to attribute this arson to a Communist conspiracy. The psychological strategy was simple and could not fail in its purpose: the burning of a public building would appear to all as the signal for a wave of terrorism, and everyone would rejoice that there was, at last, in Europe one government strong enough to hold in check criminals who stopped at nothing. The day after the crime, a Paris newspaper, Catholic, reactionary and widely read in military circles, announced the event in the very terms in which the Nazis wanted it to be announced: *The Communists have set fire to the Reichstag.* The plan had worked. Hitler was henceforth the man who had reassured the conservatives. He would still have several other chances to play this most important role . . . A few weeks later, that is, in March or April, 1933, I had with a friend a conversation that now seems to me full of symbolical meaning. He was a young man of great intelligence and of a high religious and moral character. Through his family he was in connection with the conservative aristocracy and with the most partisan section of the Catholic bourgeoisie. I received from him a foretaste of what would be the Nazi propaganda addressed to Catholics throughout the world: Hitler was the most formidable adversary of Communism, he was also an enemy of atheism and of Freemasonry; he always invoked God in his speeches, French policy was wrong in many respects, etc. And as to war, the Nazis did not want it. My friend received this information from M. Henri Massis who had recently returned from Germany. As a matter of fact, the Nazis were, for the time being, sufficiently busy with the conquest of Germany herself. It was not too difficult to spread abroad the belief that their movement was a purely domestic affair and that their military preparations were exclusively directed against Communism, the one enemy that united all honest people. And the French thought that they, too, had some serious domestic problems to settle.

The depression was becoming more and more serious and discontent was growing. A scandal provoked an explosion. In the last months of 1933 the newspapers informed the public that a great swindle had just been discovered. The author of this swindle, Stavisky, had enjoyed the protection of a considerable number of public figures. Several politicians were implicated in the affair. The Stavisky scandal was a hard blow to the Liberal party and to Freemasonry: the Rightist parties were going to exploit it to the limit. In a few weeks, the newspaper campaigns succeeded in creating an atmosphere of tragedy. Organizations of war veterans and political leagues held many demonstrations which became more and more violent. On February 6, 1934, there was, for the first time since 1871, a great and bloody riot in Paris. The political consequences of this event were incalculable. Henceforth the obsession of civil war was to prevail. The Sixth of February had proved that a civil war in France was not impossible. In the shadow of this horrifying obsession, people became panic-stricken, hatreds grew more and more bitter, the credulity of the public took on fantastic proportions, and the number of those whom fear, anger, and credulity made ready for anything, increased unceasingly.

But the most important of the immediate political results of the Sixth of February was the formation of the People's Front. Before this tragic day the Fascist peril had never been taken very seriously. On February 6th, the Fascist leagues proved they were capable of attempting a *coup d'état*; if not of succeeding in it. In the presence of such an obvious menace all the anti-Fascist forces of France understood that it was high time to put aside their dissensions and to achieve this unity of action which the anti-Fascist forces of Germany had not been able to realize when confronted by the menace of Hitlerism. The Sunday following the Sixth of February, the leader of the Communist party, Marcel Cachin, and the leader of the Socialist party, Léon Blum, harangued, one after the other, a huge crowd of workers assembled in order to affirm their resolution to defend democratic liberties against growing Fascism. Such a meeting together of the two great proletarian parties was unprecedented. But in order to understand the significance of this event and of what was then going on, we must go back to 1920.

In that year the French Socialist party split into two rival organizations. This division was brought about by the question of adherence to the Third International. To adhere to the Third International was to adhere to the Russian Revolution; it meant also, as the central committee of the International made known to the French with brutal frankness, to obey blindly the orders of the men from Moscow. The section of the Socialist party which pronounced itself in favor of adherence to the Third International took the name of Communist Party; the section which decided to remain faithful to the Second International (Amsterdam) kept the name of Socialist Party. A corresponding split took place in the labor movement between the *Unitary General Confederation of Labor* (C. G. T. U.), akin to the Communist party, and the *General Confederation of Labor* (C. G. T.), akin to the Socialist party. For long years, Socialists and Communists remained irretrievably divided. The Socialists, desirous of not showing plainly their conversion to democratic cooperation and of affirming that they remained a proletarian party, wholly dedicated to the principle of class struggle, proved rather moderate in their criticism of the Communists; but the latter, which had nothing to fear from any demagogy, never missed a chance to indulge in the most violent forms of polemics against the Socialists. Regarded with distrust by the Liberals, detested by the Rightist groups, the Socialist party had no more determined and redoubtable opponent than the Communist party. The men of the Right feigned to see little difference between Communists and Socialists; but the Rightist newspapers knew very well that to supply themselves with arguments against the Socialists, they had only to draw on the mass of denunciations constantly accumulating in the Communist papers. From time to time, a voice arose, in the Socialist world, to deplore the division of the forces of labor. Advocates of unity celebrated the memory of Jaurès, the great leader whose eloquence and cleverness had brought about the unification of French Socialism. They emphasized the advantages the enemies of the proletarian movement were gaining from the division of the proletarian forces; they suggested the idea of a *united front*. These attempts were immediately frustrated by the disdainful refusal of the Communists. Their hostility was rooted in great historical events: the vote of war appropriations by the Socialists in 1914, the ruthless repression of the Communist revolution in Germany by a Socialist government (1919). This hostility was also rooted, and perhaps still more deeply, in an incompatibility of temperaments. It was said that the Socialists were lawyers pleading a cause, while the Communists were soldiers preparing an attack. A Communist can easily become a Fascist, even more easily a Nazi; he can not become a Socialist.

But after the Sixth of February, all repugnance was immediately overcome. The two Confederations of Labor were merged together. The union of the Socialist and Communist forces became the starting point of a larger unity. The Fascist menace seemed so imminent, that the very principle of class struggle was sacrificed to the exigencies of defense against the common enemy. Contrary to all precedent, the Communist party went so far as to agree to collaboration with the Liberal party, a bourgeois organization par excellence, and even sought this collaboration. A fraction of the Liberal party agreed to enter into a coalition with the two great proletarian parties. And this is how the People's Front was formed—a heterogeneous collection in which men like Daladier, Herriot, and Blum, whom the Communists had insulted daily for fifteen years, consented to form with these same Communists a mass united "like the fingers of the hand."[12]

Many things could be said about the petty intrigues which contributed to the formation of the People's Front. Let us rather consider what the newly born People's Front represented in the opinion of the French masses. After years of helplessness, of almost silent anguish, of exhausting misery, of scepticism and despair, the formation of the People's Front succeeded in arousing, for a rather short time, a wave of hope. It was doubtlessly very unreasonable to expect any enduring achievement from this combination, made up of bourgeois terrified by the idea of social revolution, of hesitating Socialists, and of Communists whom everybody knew to be capable of every ruse, every kind of violence and sabotage, and totally submissive to the Stalin government. But the need for believing and hoping, after these years of fatalistic resignation and of dreary suffering, was stronger than any rational anticipation. In the twilight of

[12] The *closed fist* was originally the symbol of that unity.

the myths, an ephemeral myth had sprung up, the myth of the People's Front which was going to provide all workers, God knows by what miracle, with bread, peace and liberty.

The more you ponder over the catastrophes of our time, the more you are led to recognize in them the *phenomena of despair*. Germany delivered herself to the Nazis in an act of despair. There is something singularly tragic in the fact that the French people, before descending, in their turn, into the great night, wished to indulge, one last time, and at the price of fantastic illusions, in the belief that the happiness of living and of being free could still be enjoyed on the soil of France.

VI

Our Friends' Friends Are Our Friends

During the first World War, every attack was preceded by an artillery preparation, a costly operation the results of which were often uncertain. Hitler has declared that the role of artillery preparation would henceforth be played by propaganda. Let us always keep well in mind this formula of Hitler; it throws a strong light on the genesis of today's calamities and the nature of the menace which hangs over the last free countries.

Propaganda can be carried on frankly and openly. Even under these conditions it has a redoubtable effectiveness because of the great number of fools who instinctively believe that anything printed is true, or at least contains, as they say, a basis of truth. But by concealing itself propaganda can overcome many obstacles before which an open propaganda would fail. It used to be said that the English Parliament could do everything except change a man into a woman; that is about the only thing that skillfully camouflaged propaganda cannot do. The defeat of France proves this abundantly.

Although France, at the time Hitler came into power, was seriously weakened by internal crises, no open propaganda in favor of Hitler's Germany could have been imposed on the French public. Yet Hitler had to break the morale of the French; otherwise he would himself be destroyed by the dynamism which drove the Nazi party to attempt the enslavement of the world after having achieved the enslavement of Germany. For France had still an overwhelming military superiority over Germany; she had powerful and faithful allies; she had all the necessary legal instruments to prevent German rearmament. She had only to will it. The slightest resistance on the part of France would have found powerful support from within Germany. Nazism had no chance to inflict its New Order upon Europe and the world unless it first succeeded in stultifying the will of the French people.

Such a task might seem impossible. A German general said that the French would never give up the demilitarization of the Rhineland unless they were compelled to by a crushing defeat. But a military defeat of France could not possibly be accomplished, nor even attempted, so long as the Rhineland was demilitarized. This general thought he was caught in a vicious circle. He was wrong. Subsequent events were to prove that it was possible to weaken the moral resistance of the French to such an extent that they would be willing to give up, one after another, all the guarantees of security they had been given by treaties.

From the point of view of foreign policy it can be said with sufficient accuracy that France was then divided into a section dominated by nationalist groups and a section dominated by socialist groups. It would be an absurd oversimplification to assert that every Frenchman was either a nationalist or a socialist, but the political opinions of the French, in matters of foreign policy, were actually polarized on the one hand by Nationalism, on the other by Socialism. Of course these two words are used in a very broad sense.

Here attention must be called to a point of decisive importance. It is inevitable, and to a certain extent perfectly normal, that the people most interested in national defence are those who are the least interested in social progress; whereas the people who are the most interested in social progress are those least interested in national defence. This division of labor is not simply the result of temperamental differences: it derives from a real conflict between the ends which are pursued. Social progress, whether real or illusory, is expensive; national defence is expensive also. It is natural that each category of expenditure should have its habitual supporters. Moreover, the institutions which foster social progress, whether real or illusory, are not always the most favorable to national defence and vice versa. All goes as well as possible when the balance is maintained between the forces of social progress and those of national defence. All is jeopardized if party-spirit prevails on either side; if the advocates of social progress refuse the most necessary sacrifices for national defence and if the advocates of national defence refuse any concession to the demands of social progress. But the worst happens when one of the two groups becomes unfaithful to its vocation and abandons its role. The role thus abandoned will not be taken up by anybody else, for the other group is absolutely incapable of assuming it in addition to its own, or of substituting it for its own. If the nationalist groups fail in their duty of providing for national defence, it is certain that nobody will provide for it.

Now this is what happened to France: owing to a complicated set of circumstances, and to a lot of maneuvering and connivance, the French nationalists were led to abandon their role as guardians of the city. If the Socialists had been perfectly clear-sighted, resolute and disinterested, they would still have been unable to accomplish the work of national salvation which all historical forces had entrusted to other hands. As a matter of fact, they were far from being perfectly clear-sighted, resolute and disinterested.

Let us imagine the fiction (devoid of any historical likelihood) of a republican and socialist Germany planning an aggression against France, and determined to use, according to Hitler's formula, propaganda as a kind of artillery preparation. Her propaganda would naturally have been addressed to the French Socialists. They are the ones whom Germany would have tried to convince that nothing was threatening the independence of the French nation. It is through them that she would have tried to lead France into a policy of unwise concessions. She would have endeavored to induce them to increase their demands for costly reforms at the expense of military appropriations. The success of such strategy would have been dubious, since the nationalist party would not have failed to play its role as defender of national interests against the Socialists blind to the dangers threatening the nation.

Hitler could not adopt this strategy. French Socialists, and Socialists all over the world, had too many reasons to hate Nazism. To whom then was Nazi propaganda in France to be addressed? The reader may be inclined to believe that if the observations set forth in Chapter II are exact, all German propaganda addressed to French Nationalists was doomed to certain failure. But here is the great paradox: while the British Parliament was never able to change a man into a woman, propaganda proved able to transform the majority of the French Nationalists into irresolute people, quite a number of French Nationalists into sympathizers, and a handful of French Nationalists into traitors. The secret of such a bewildering change? Above all, the skillful use of intermediaries. It was not impossible for Hitler to gain many friends among the French on condition that he use his friends as go-betweens. It was not impossible for Hitler to win the sympathy of a good number of Frenchmen provided that a good number of Frenchmen would become the friends of his friends. For our friends' friends are our friends.

Germany was still in the early stages of her intensive rearmament when another dictator-state made known to the world its will for aggression: during the spring and summer of 1935 it became plain that Italy was going to attempt the conquest of Ethiopia.

The French had many reasons to oppose this undertaking. It was their duty to oppose it, first of all, because it was a manifestly unjust war. The question which then confronted the Christian conscience was this: would the teaching of the Church on the war be taken seriously,[13] or would it be assumed that this teaching was a merely theoretical and academic matter, useful for exercising the argumentative minds of students of theology, but irrevocably destined never to save a people from the horrors of an unjust war. Whoever has pondered over the problems of the moral life knows how easy it is for the dishonest conscience to elude

[13] Let us recall here the strong statement of His Holiness **Pope Pius XI**. (Address at Castel Gandolfo, Sept., 1935.)

the most sacred truths and to render them powerless without taking the trouble to openly reject them. The application of moral principles is often difficult and obscure. It requires a discrimination which the honest conscience alone can achieve. A dishonest conscience is never embarrassed. Why bother, for example, to attack openly the doctrine of the Church on the just price? Greedy merchants will always have plenty of good reasons to prove that their profits conform perfectly with the laws of the just price. These arguments will be specious enough to convince the many weak-willed people who prefer not to examine the case too closely, lest they discover the iniquity within their own consciences. Likewise, why bother to declare openly that one rejects the teaching of the Church on the conditions of the just war, and that one makes a mockery of justice with regard to it or anything else? It is much more clever to profit by the obscurities which inevitably accompany the application of a necessarily abstract doctrine. Using darkness as a protection! This is a method familiar to all marauders, pickpockets and assassins. In most cases the obscurity of the application offers sufficient protection to the scoundrels. But there are typical cases where the application is comparatively clear; then the light of the doctrine itself becomes embarrassing and the only solution is to pass over the doctrine in silence. The encyclical *Divini Redemptoris* mentions that some employers objected to the encyclical *Quadragesimo anno* being read publicly in their parishes. I have been told that at the time of the Ethiopian war a professor of theology in a Roman college felt very uneasy, because his course included the theory of the just war. He spoke of it to his superior who decided that the state of public opinion would not permit the treatment of so burning a question. All that can be said of such an omission is that it was incomparably less dishonest than the historical and doctrinal falsifications which had to be effected if the Fascist aggression was to be given the slightest appearance of justification.

The French had a very particular reason to oppose the Fascist aggression in Ethiopia. It was clear that the success of this aggression would mean the complete collapse of the system of collective security which France had such an interest in strengthening. At the time the Italo-Ethiopian crisis began, the League of Nations had already experienced some resounding failures: the war in Manchuria (1932), the withdrawal of Japan, and the withdrawal of Germany. Yet some recent events had given it a rather unexpected recovery of prestige: it had received the adherence of Russia in 1934; it had successfully settled the quarrel between Hungary and Jugoslavia (1935); it had maintained peace in the Saar district at the time of the plebiscite (January, 1935). But above all, the League of Nations was supported at the time by an extremely favorable public opinion in Britain. A poll made by private organizations, the *Peace Ballot*, had shown that the great majority of the British people had made up their minds in favor of a policy of complete fidelity to the Covenant, going so far as to envisage the use of military sanctions. After a long and deplorable period of indecision, Great Britain showed herself determined to abandon her traditional policy of isolation and to commit herself fully in European and world affairs. But she wanted her commitments to have the character of a participation in a system of collective assistance. The League of Nations in 1935 was strong enough to stop dead the attempted aggression of the Fascists. On the other hand, it could not withstand another large-scale failure. The Italo-Ethiopian conflict was to be the decisive test; the enemies of international law understood this perfectly.

In addition to the obligation of defending justice and of assuring the triumph of international order, the French had a vital interest in not separating their policy from that of Great Britain, their indispensable ally in a possible war with Nazi Germany, whose military power was increasing daily. Now, the era of the ill-fated policy of appeasement had not yet begun; British statesmen, supported by an almost unanimous popular movement, had understood the meaning of the aggression launched by Italy against a people without airplanes and without artillery. They had understood that the establishment of a Fascist empire in East Africa would inevitably create a formidable and perhaps fatal threat to the route to the Indies and the British positions in the Eastern Mediterranean. At the time I write these lines a hard battle is raging in Libya; what is happening today was foreseen as early as 1935. Those who are astonished that some Frenchmen are trying to drag France into the struggle against Great Britain are ignorant of contemporary history. They know nothing of the decisive events which took place in 1935 and 1936.

The foreign policy of France was controlled by Laval, whose character has been completely revealed by recent developments. To those who considered only the official attitude of the French government, it might seem that its policy was wholly true to its engagements under the Covenant. Before the beginning of hostilities, Laval joined his efforts to those of the British government in order to secure a peaceful settlement. Once the Italian aggression started, the Council of the League of Nations, in which France had a permanent seat, unanimously declared that Italy had had recourse to war contrary to her promises; in the Assembly of the League France shared in the unanimous vote in favor of the application of sanctions.

But nobody ever believed in the sincerity of this official policy. Laval was known to be a friend of Fascist Italy and his being in power seemed quite reassuring to those who had undertaken to sabotage international order. Friends and adversaries of Laval recognized that thanks to him sanctions had become a farce. These sanctions would have been effective in a long war, but the Fascists did not need a long war. Their aviators, by an extensive use of mustard gas, opened a road to Addis Ababa, and their columns went forward amidst the corpses; then Mussolini appeared once more on the balcony of the Palazzo Venezia, and declared that the war was over. The Ethiopian war was not over, but the first objective of the dictators was reached: henceforth Europe was disorganized, demoralized, and they had no longer anything to fear from collective security.

Laval is nothing more than a politician of the lowest order, a corporation lawyer, a clever schemer who made a lot of money. The interesting thing to consider is the reaction of the French public to the challenge of the Ethiopian war to justice, international order and the security of all nations. Few persons were so stupid as to fail to recognize the seriousness of the event; France split into supporters and adversaries of the League of Nations just as she had split, thirty-five years earlier, into supporters and adversaries of Captain Dreyfus. The adversaries of Mussolini were the men of the newly formed People's Front, and a great number of Catholics. The Right, the conservatives and reactionaries, the nationalist party, whose members I have described as the *guardians of the city*, stood up almost unanimously[14] against the League of Nations, against international law, and against the treaties signed by France; they supported the Italian aggression with a feverish enthusiasm. The excuse they offered to patriots was that opposition to the ambitions of Fascist Italy would force her into an alliance with Germany. In fact, a resolute action against the Fascist ag-

[14] I mean that there were very few exceptions. See below.

gression would have simply brought about the downfall of Mussolini's regime and the emergence of a republican Italy in which Nazi Germany could not have found an ally. This is precisely what they wanted to avoid at any price: the overthrow of this Fascist regime which they considered so much better than the French Republic —a regime which they had vainly tried to establish in France, and which they would someday succeed in establishing through the defeat of the French armies. In any case the desire of maintaining friendly relations with Italy could neither justify nor explain the enthusiasm with which this obviously unjust and cruel war was cheered by the Rightist parties and their sympathizers. Their zeal was above all a tribute to triumphant force, consistently accompanied by a diabolical irony in which were combined a contempt for the pledged word, a hate of juridical forms, and an exaltation of violent passions at the expense of justice and mercy.

Patriotic considerations carried little weight amidst this explosion of wicked instincts. The few members of the Right who raised their voices in protest against the Italian aggression, either for moral reasons (François Mauriac) or for patriotic reasons (Pertinax, Buré) were soon disavowed by their parties, or left them in disgust. The Ethiopian war did more than anything else to determine many Catholics to break their traditional ties with the Right. These Catholics were to become the object of bitter resentment. A bishop told one of them a few years later: "They have not forgiven you your Christian attitude with regard to the Ethiopian war."

We witnessed then a strange orgy of vile passions. A large part of the press was obviously bought by the Italian government. To reinforce its propaganda, a group of well known intellectuals, including a goodly number of stars from the French Academy, published a manifesto boldly entitled *For the Defence of the West*. As the title suggests, this manifesto contained nothing but lies and nonsense, but the authority of the signers could not fail to impress a great number of ill-informed and cowardly people. Those who but recently were the most willing to recall the German atrocities of 1914 had no objection to the extermination of the Ethiopian populace with mustard gas. Those who but recently recalled with indignation the expression of Chancellor Bethman-Hollweg, who called the treaty guaranteeing Belgian neutrality "a scrap of paper," viewed with sympathy the action of the Fascist government tearing up three or four scraps of paper in order to carry on in Ethiopia its war of "civilization."[15]

I have tried to point out in the preceding pages the three great reasons why the French should have unanimously opposed the Ethiopian war: justice, collective assistance, and Anglo-French co-operation were at stake. These were so many reasons why the French Right was to favor the Ethiopian war. Justice seemed to it an abstract and suspicious idea. It hated the League of Nations. It hated England. The great campaign of insult hurled against England by its newspapers was the logical complement to its campaign in favor of the Fascists. It was the time when the pamphleteer Henri Béraud published in *Gringoire* articles entitled "Why I Hate the English," "Should England be Reduced to Slavery?" etc. Five years later, in his address announcing the Armistice, Marshal Pétain pointed out that France had not had enough

[15] It is interesting to re-read the speech in which Bethman-Hollweg announced to the Reichstag the invasion of Belgium in 1914, and to compare it with the manifesto *For the Defence of the West*. Compared with the average member of the French Academy, Bethman-Hollweg appears as a man of scrupulous conscience. He took the trouble to recognize that the violation of Belgian neutrality was contrary to law. He took the trouble to express the intention of repairing the injustice which necessity, as he called it, compelled him to commit. The "defenders of the West" did not bother about such scruples. They were already ripe in 1935 for the policy of "collaboration" with the Nazis.

allies. Everyone recognized in this statement a bitter criticism of England. But the Marshal could not afford to say that his most fervent supporters were among the men who, in regard to the question of war debts, plastered all over Paris posters demanding *"Not a cent for America,"* and who, in regard to the Ethiopian war, spoke of reducing England to slavery. This point must be made perfectly clear: the policy of stabbing England in the back, which is practiced today by Admiral Darlan, is only the fulfillment of a sort of oath taken in an atmosphere of hatred by the French Right in 1935.

The fate of Europe was sealed in 1935-1936. Everything happened as if the enemies of peace had accepted the fundamental assumption of the defenders of international institutions, namely, that international order could be guaranteed by a system of collective assistance and only by such a system. Owing to the sabotage of the League of Nations, a new era was about to begin in which law would no longer be made by assemblies of jurists, but by the force of arms, as in Ethiopia. Toward the end of 1935 the Parisian magazine *Le Document* published a special issue devoted to the pressing problem of rearmament. On the first page was an article accompanied by a picture of a cloudy sky. The title was "We have lived for fifteen years in the clouds." For fifteen years Europe had been spared from exhausting herself in military expenditures. The article showed that this period had come to an end, and that in the new era which was beginning, force was to play a much greater part. The author frankly rejoiced over this change in international mores. *We have lived for fifteen years in the clouds:* owing to universal rearmament life was to begin again in earnest. The author of the article was General Weygand.

But what would happen if France were outdistanced by rival nations in a world rearmament race? It could not be said that such a possibility was out of the question, but it was suggested that there could be no serious danger as long as the strong men in whom the nationalist party had placed its confidence remained in power. Who were these trusted men? Let us imagine the following parlor game: in 1935 or 1936 some people well-informed about political conditions amuse themselves in drawing up, each one by himself, a list of the political men who have the confidence of "nationalist France." These lists would have varied considerably, because the real answer was not clear. But one name at least would have appeared on all of them, that of Laval.

OUR FRIENDS' FRIENDS

No doubt it was vaguely realized that *in fact* the balance of military power had a great chance of being broken to the disadvantage of France: but it was known also that *in fact* the "nationalist" party and Laval would not always remain in power. Thus, should a catastrophe occur, they would in any case have the consolation of saying that it was the fault of the Socialists, and that everything would have turned out differently if instead of trusting "this dirty Blum," France had kept on being guided by the wonderful Monsieur Laval. I know some Frenchmen who did not fail to relish this consolation after the defeat.

VII

The People's Front in Power

THE People's Front won in the election of May, 1936. Its victory, although impressive, did not give it complete security against possible waverings of parliamentary opinion. For a shift of sixty Liberal votes would suffice to put the People's Front government in a minority in the Chamber of Deputies. The great majority of the Senate was hostile to the People's Front. Besides the colossal difficulties resulting from the social, economic and international conditions, the new government would soon have to meet all the difficulties that a powerful parliamentary opposition would not fail to provoke. There are democratic countries where the defeated parties accept with good grace the victory of their adversary, while hoping for better success in the next elections. In France on the contrary, the party which has suffered an electoral defeat considers that not all is lost, because there still remains the possibility of hamstringing, intriguing and sabotaging the work of the victor's administration.

Nothing was so striking in the results of the 1936 elections as the progress made by the Communist group. From the foundation of the Communist party in 1920 until 1936 the Communists had never had more than twenty-five to thirty representatives in the Chamber, sometimes much less. It was a noisy minority which annoyed everybody, but played only a negligible part in the passing of bills and in the control of the administration's policy. The elections of 1936 sent seventy-two Communist deputies[16] to the Chamber. To understand the meaning of this change we must bear in mind the characteristics of the French electoral system. It was a compromise between the majority system and proportional representation. The candidate who wins an absolute majority at the first ballot is elected. If no candidate wins an absolute

[16] The Chamber had 618 members.

majority a second ballot takes place, and this time the election is won by the candidate who obtains the relative majority of the votes. When several parties form an electoral coalition each party presents a candidate on the first ballot; on the second ballot the candidates who had the least votes withdraw in favor of the one who has gained the most votes. In the 1936 elections, very few Communists were elected on the first ballot; most of them owed their election to the support of Socialist and Liberal voters on the second ballot. The success of the Communists in the elections of 1936 meant no doubt an increase in the number of Communists throughout France. But it meant, above all, an uncompromising will to achieve the union of all the so-called Leftist forces against Fascism.

The Socialist party was the principal victor. The Communists refused to share the responsibility of power. The first cabinet to face the new Chamber was a combination of Socialists and Liberals in which the Socialists predominated. The Prime Minister was the general secretary of the Socialist party, Léon Blum. He had never been a member of the government. At the time of the *Cartel des Gauches* (1924) the Socialist party supported its Liberal allies without being represented in the Cabinet. Ever since then, Léon Blum had been one of the most bitterly criticized and hated of French politicians. The Rightist press had tirelessly pictured him as an inscrutable figure, secretly engineering nefarious intrigues which were allegedly carried out by others. A few months before the elections Blum had been badly mauled by members of the *Action Française*. He was known as a highly cultured man, a great connoisseur of belles-lettres, who wrote perfect Latin, an artist, a wealthy man, a representative of a Parisian aristocracy among which esthetic refinement is sometimes accompanied by revolutionary tendencies. He was said to have an extraordinary intelligence. At the time he assumed power, Blum enjoyed an enormous popularity among Leftist circles and among the masses. It would have been difficult to cite evidence of his political ability. Yet many people were seduced by the prestige of his culture and also by the idealistic fervor of this sixty-five year old artist whom French democracy, in a supreme outburst of hope, had entrusted with giving France "peace, bread, and liberty" amidst unfolding world catastrophes. This popularity overflowed among circles hostile to the People's Front. I shall never forget the conviction with which an elderly lady, who had always read only Rightist newspapers, forgot for a while everything she had read and repeated for twelve years about "this dirty Blum," and declared to me that France would be saved by the great intelligence of the new Prime Minister.

One of the characteristics of the electoral campaign of 1936 was that anti-clerical propaganda played little or no role in it. Yet the parties which composed the bulk of the People's Front numbered almost exclusively unbelievers, and many of their members had formerly participated in anti-clerical struggles. All those who know the history of modern France, particularly those who witnessed the anti-clerical outburst of 1924, will agree that this was an event of considerable significance, and would like to know the reasons for it.

The People's Front was, as we have seen, a coalition embracing, in addition to the proletarian parties, a section of the Liberal middle class. The Liberal middle class had been for several generations the very soul of anti-clericalism. The anti-religious laws of the beginning of the century were above all the work of anti-clerical middle class people whose chief political organization was the Liberal party. In the but recent past, anti-clericalism was the most common and unshakable element of liberal doctrine. What had happened to the anti-clerical middle class by 1936? *Broadly speak-*

ing, it had become conservative. It had become conservative because it had remained middle class minded at a time when revolution had become proletarian or plebeian. For more than fifty years the Liberal party had showed itself faithful to the battle-cry of Gambetta: *Clericalism, that is the enemy*. But as early as 1927 or 1928, Sarraut, one of the veterans of the Liberal party, sounded the note of a new spirit when he launched this parody of Gambetta: *Communism, that is the enemy.* Against Communism, and possibly also against the growing power of trade unions, the overwhelming majority of the Liberals felt disposed to ally themselves with all anti-revolutionary forces, not excepting the Catholic Church. After all, on close examination—it was no doubt the first time in their lives they examined the question attentively—they realized that they no longer had any reason to detest the Catholic Church.

What I do not hesitate to write on the fundamental anti-communism of most Liberals may seem in contradiction with the fact that by joining the People's Front coalition, some of the Liberals had agreed to collaborate with the Communists, and even advised their supporters to vote for the Communist candidates, if necessary, on the second ballot. This is a paradox which can easily be explained by circumstances of the moment which had no relation to the general evolution of the middle class and of the Liberal party. After the Stavisky affair and the riots of February 6th, 1934, the Rightist newspapers launched an incredibly savage campaign against several Liberal leaders (Daladier and Chautemps in particular). It was said that this campaign could be compared only to the anti-semitic ravings of the Nazi *Der Sturmer*. The outraged men gained their revenge at the price of an electoral coalition. They represented only a portion of the Liberal party. As soon as the People's Front suffered its first setbacks, they rejoined the anti-Communist policy to which their party was becoming more and more attached. They were the very men who liquidated the People's Front. Once the war had begun, they suppressed the Communist party and arrested many of its members,—while they did not bother to arrest the traitors of the pro-Fascist faction.

Giving up anti-clericalism was for the Liberals the more easy since their ideology was dead. Middle class anti-clericalism was bound up with the prevalence of a rationalistic, naturalistic and essentially optimistic philosophy in which nobody any longer believed. Let us mention, finally, that the anti-clericalism of the rural population, among which the Liberals recruited many voters, had, in the past, been stimulated by economic motives that no longer existed and were being forgotten. Less than twenty years ago, a man who knew the rural world very well called my attention to the persistence of an anti-clerical mood in a region with a large majority of practicing Catholics. This paradoxical disposition could be accounted for, according to him, by the fact that these people still remembered the already distant time when the clergy were rich and cost a great deal to maintain. This traditional resentment could not long survive the example of admirable poverty which the French clergy has given in our time, particularly since the first World War. It is surely moving to realize that the weakening of anti-clerical prejudice in the French countryside has been the reward of the poverty so generously accepted by many humble priests.

As for the industrial workers, the situation was dominated by the new policy of the Communist party, one of the most strange events in a period replete with astonishing developments. Until 1934 the atheistic philosophy of the Communist party in France, as well as elsewhere, had always been accompanied by an anti-clerical policy which surpassed in violence and vulgarity anything that the

Liberals and Socialists dared to use. The first evidences of an entirely unexpected change appeared in the spring of 1934. *L'Humanité* published a speech by Maurice Thorez, General Secretary of the Party, which had as subtitles these two catch-phrases without precedent in the history of the party: *We love our country . . . No policy of systematic violence against religion.* . . . Two years later the same Thorez in an electoral broadcast launched the famous slogan: "Catholics, we offer you the outstretched hand." At first it was considered only a campaign maneuver, but in the following months, and as late as two years after the electoral victory of the People's Front, every Communist speech, even if given by a village politician, included inevitably a development of *the outstretched hand*. Occasionally the speaker took the trouble to recall that the party remained atheist, and then the public felt completely confused. But in most cases they avoided calling attention to the philosophy of the party. *L'Humanité* cited with praise the generous undertakings of Cardinal Verdier. In some industrial towns, the Communist mayor was delighted to facilitate the functioning of social agencies directed by parish priests. Finally Maurice Thorez gave a speech in the Chamber which, if it meant anything at all, meant that the

Communist party was about to demand that the right to teach be legally restored to religious orders. Forced to explain himself, he made it known that his speech did not signify anything at all. The fact remained that a trial balloon had been sent up.

No serious observer ever believed for an instant that all these astounding demonstrations could mean that there had been any change in the fundamental and necessary opposition of the Communist party to religion. The whole thing was simply a farce, yet the idea behind such an unexpected farce had to be explained. To our knowledge, the only possible explanation is that the Communists hoped, by the policy of *the outstretched hand*, to increase their influence among the lower middle class and the rural population. They certainly failed. But the very fact that they attempted such a maneuver bears a most impressive evidence of the revival of religion among the French masses. Twenty years earlier such an effort to curry the favor of the Catholics could only have harmed a revolutionary party anxious to win over the rural world and the lower middle class. It would have provoked a violent opposition among industrial workers. Nothing had been changed in the real dispositions of the Communists, but something had been changed in the dispositions of the French people. This is what was proved by the incident of the outstretched hand.

It was in the Socialist party that the anti-clerical traditions of the French Left proved most resistant. More than once the Socialist press manifested how little confidence it had in the neo-clericalism of the Communists. Yet even among the Socialists, passions which were still alive were partly silenced, or bound to express themselves discreetly; this was due to the general dispositions of public opinion, the decadence of humanitarian ideology, and also, in some cases, to a confused nostalgia for the living sources of justice and peace. A certain amount of anti-religious activity took place in French politics during the years of the People's Front. It is significant that it was bound to proceed surreptitiously. It was chiefly the work of a few fanatics in key positions who, by decrees and instructions hardly known to the public, could impress upon national education a trend hostile to the Church.

It was during the regime of the People's Front that some of the most moving manifestations of the religious revival in France took place. Léon Blum was Prime Minister when the rumor spread that Pope Pius XI wished to attend in person the ceremonies at Lisieux in honor of St. Theresa of the Child Jesus. He declared that the only place where France could decently receive the Pope was the Chateau of Versailles, and he immediately ordered the necessary preparations to be planned. The illness of Pius XI deprived history of an event which would not only have been colorful, but really sublime: the French Republic, which so often had sinned against the Papacy, receiving triumphantly the Vicar of Jesus Christ in the Palace of Louis XIV. Cardinal Pacelli, the papal legate at Lisieux, was accorded royal honors. It was also during the regime of the People's Front that the Congress of the Young Christian Workers (J.O.C.) was held,—certainly the greatest collective demonstration of Catholic faith ever given by the proletarian class on the soil of France.

A few weeks after these two great events (1937), which I was unable to witness, I happened to be at the *Semaine Sociale* (Social Week) in Clermont-Ferrand. The *Semaines Sociales* are annual congresses where Catholics of all social conditions assemble to discuss present-day social problems. Many of those there had assisted at the ceremonies in Lisieux and at the Congress of the J.O.C., both of which had left them deeply moved. The Nuncio was one of these witnesses, and he did not fail to give enthusiastic expression to his confidence in the destiny of Christian France. Now, I had the pleasure of meeting at the *Semaine Sociale* in Clermont-Ferrand an Italian priest with whom I had become acquainted the year before. He was an entertaining man, and to amuse me, told me that as he was about to leave Italy, his confreres had advised him to take with him some layman's clothes, for in the France of the People's Front, a priest in clerical garments had a good chance of being lynched. This story was the more amusing since the *Semaine Sociale* had attracted many priests to Clermont-Ferrand, an old industrial and socialist center, and the city was black with cassocks. Another story current during the Congress was that, a few months earlier, a very high Roman dignitary, arriving in Paris and finding at the station a group of prelates who had come to welcome him, exclaimed: "What imprudence!" For he, too, believed that in France a man in cassock was running a great risk. Yet it was not difficult to know in Italy what could be seen in the streets of French cities. The meaning of such gossip was quite clear: there were people who made Catholics abroad believe that France had become another Spain, and that religion in France was suffering a bloody persecution. Stories of this kind were first carried to Rome to be sure that the whole world would hear them. It is hard to say who were the people who started these lies, but it is not hard to say for whom they were working. Any lie capable of smearing the religious situation in France was an effective contribution to the legend which was to lure so many Catholics all over the world into an insane policy of connivance with the Nazis.[17]

The Blum cabinet had not yet held its first meeting when a social development of large proportions took place throughout France. Strikes broke out everywhere and these strikes were accompanied by a new phenomenon, the occupation of the factories by the strikers. The first act of the Blum government was the quick conclusion of an agreement between labor and management. Then Parliament was asked to pass a series of social laws.

[17] An enormous fault of Léon Blum helped to feed this propaganda. In his youth, Blum had written a book on marriage, the immorality of which recalls the writings of Bertrand Russell. The book had been forgotten by the public and it was very desirable that it remain so. While he was Prime Minister, Blum, with incredible foolishness, permitted, or urged, the publication of a new French edition and an English translation of it. I have no disposition to throw stones at anybody and I willingly recognize that if God had not given me the grace to be born in a Christian family, my ethical ideas might have been as false as those of Blum. But even if he had no knowledge of moral truth, the Prime Minister should have been prevented by simple decency from inflicting on the French people the shame of this new edition and this translation.

The occupation of factories by the strikers was rightly considered as an event of major importance in the evolution of labor relations. Some viewed them mostly as an unjustifiable violation of the right of property, others viewed them as an anticipation of a new juridical regime. It was surely an anticipation of a new regime of industrial property, but this anticipation involved an unquestionable offence against property as determined by the existing state of things. The historical importance of the event, its extent, and its novelty make more striking the fact that it caused relatively few disorders. There was no doubt some violence here and there, but the most astonishing thing is that there was so little of it. The general impression was that the operation was carried out with discipline. In most cases the strikers were careful to prevent the deterioration of the machinery. Besides some disturbing stories, some moving ones were told: how members of the J.O.C. received the Blessed Sacrament in workshops while their fellow workers observed a respectful attitude; how the Catholic employees of a big department store were allowed to leave it in order to attend Mass and how they returned immediately after Mass; how some strikers, having to send a delegation to the Ministry of Labor, called politely on their employer to ask permission to use one of the factory cars, etc. A few months later, all talk about sit-down strikes, except in revolutionary circles, was indignant and bitter. It is very remarkable that at the time the great wave of strikes took place (June 1936), they were considered by the public without too much opposition and sometimes even with an almost friendly patience. Many persons traditionally hostile to labor's demands understood that a general wage increase was indispensable, that the time had come to give the workers more security, and finally that more leisure for the largest and poorest class was a normal and happy result of economic evolution. As to the violation of property, public anger was tempered by the confused feeling that capital could not everlastingly claim exclusive ownership of the tools of production.

In our opinion, any evaluation of the social laws which were then passed in a great hurry should be carefully balanced. One thing is certain: they were not revolutionary measures, and they might well have been introduced by a Catholic democratic government. It has often been said that, in themselves and apart from the circumstances, they were excellent. I would not go that far. There was certainly this wrong with them, their uniformity. The clauses concerning the forty hour week in particular, whether or not practicable in large scale industries, were a fatal blow to innumerable small employers. But much more serious was the moment chosen to enforce reforms so extensive that they could not help slowing down production during a rather long period of adjustment. On the eve of a war in which equipment was to play a decisive part, this slowing down of production was nothing short of disastrous. This was no doubt vaguely realized. Yet there was a widespread feeling of resignation, because many people were convinced that these reforms were long overdue, and that they could not be further postponed. On the whole, the prevailing feeling was a mixture of fatalism and optimism: a most dangerous combination characterizing the periods of respite which come between unfolding catastrophes.

Maybe the damage would not have been so serious, if, after the great strikes and the passing of the new social laws, the industrial world had enjoyed the long period of tranquillity it so badly needed after such a change in labor relations. But in the months which followed the enforcement of the new legislation, a new series of strikes broke out in almost all parts of France. These strikes looked quite different from those which had accompanied the coming to power of the People's Front. The June strikes were clearly intended to produce such pressure as to prevent Parliament from stopping the reform movement; their meaning was plain, and they were generally carried out with some sort of order. On the contrary, the later strikes looked disorderly, chaotic and unexplainable. While observing one of them closely, I thought of those wars of the eighteenth century in which peoples, on either side, exhausted themselves without knowing why they had to undergo such suffering and destruction. From the fall of 1936 until the liquidation of the People's Front in 1938, everything happened as if some people in key positions had done their utmost to create, in the industrial life of France, a state of confusion, restlessness, anxiety and inefficiency. The important question is to know who these people were. It is not easy to give an answer. In all likelihood, several nefarious influences were at work, but it does not seem possible to say how far their action was consciously unified. The Communists, since the merger of the two Federations of Labor (1934), enjoyed a growing power in labor unions, and it is not doubtful that they used it to do a great deal of harm. Yet it is difficult to admit that they organized the sabotage of French production as early as 1936. This hypothesis would imply, what is quite improbable, that the Soviet government had already given up its policy of resistance to Nazi Germany. Trotskyites and freelance revolutionaries were often mentioned as possible authors of some particularly mysterious disorders. This oversimple explanation may have been true in some cases. There is every reason to believe that the agents of the dictatorships were numerous and active. Finally the hypothesis of sabotage by certain employers cannot be excluded. A few months after the People's Front came into power, a considerable part of the bourgeoisie cherished the desire of humiliating and crushing, at no matter what price, its hated enemy. It is impossible to understand anything of what took place in France in the last few years and is taking place there today, unless it is realized that during the last prewar years a whole class of people grew up, for whom the supremely important thing was neither money, nor honor, nor pleasure, nor God, but hatred. The starvation rations, the lack of coal, the heel of the Nazi boot and the enslavement of the nation itself are things they can stand, since such little inconveniences are counter-balanced by a most delightful experience: the complete crushing of the enemy. For certain Frenchmen are today in a triumphant mood. They are those for whom the enemy was not so much Nazi Germany as the People's Front.

At the beginning of the People's Front period, the bourgeois opposition had been weakened by the subtle influence of popular enthusiasm, and much more by astonishment. But soon the general situation became extremely favorable for the working of a ruthless opposition. Discontent was universal. The cost of living increased more rapidly than wages. None of the new social laws succeeded in functioning smoothly. Red tape multiplied endlessly, strikes broke out again and again, the instability of the currency caused panic among the lower middle class. Even those who had first trusted the People's Front no longer concealed the fact that they were tired of it. Collaboration with the Communists proved impracticable; the incompetence of the Socialist leaders in financial matters was no longer contested by anybody. The myth was dead. The hour of vengeance was nearing. For the sit-down strikes through which the imperialism of the proletariat had boldly held in check the supremacy of capitalist ownership, vengeance was demanded. For this system of collective bargaining which gave labor relations the character of contracts freely debated between equals, vengeance was demanded. For the unprecedented event of the Socialist party in power, vengeance was demanded. For the financial measures of the People's Front, whether just or absurd, vengeance was demanded. For the fear that had been felt and for the humiliations endured, vengeance was demanded.

When Léon Blum formed the first People's Front cabinet, it was noticed that the appointment of the Minister of Foreign Affairs was delayed. Foreign policy was one of the subjects in which the People's Front was most divided. According to the deplorable practice of coalition governments, a colorless figure was chosen: M. Yvon Delbos was the first Foreign Minister of the People's Front. He was a rather insignificant member of the Liberal party. Let us try to describe the various trends of foreign policy prevailing in 1936 amongst the parties composing the People's Front.

In the Liberal group, there were some patriots who at heart remained faithful to the Jacobin tradition: they were tired, worn out, very much depressed by the feeling that their tradition belonged to another age and that their ideology had been made powerless by the irrepressible developments of the present time. Other Liberals, probably the majority of them, favored what was soon to be called the appeasement policy: a policy of endless concessions to the aggressor states, a policy of encouragement to aggression, a policy of cowardice and stupid naïveté. A short time later, these defeatists of the Liberal party became indistinguishable from the defeatists of the Right. History will see little difference between Bonnet, a Liberal, a wealthy lawyer, the man of Munich, and Pierre Laval, the man in whom the Right had placed its confidence, a wealthy lawyer also, a friend of Mussolini, the man who saved Fascism in 1935. As far as we can judge, the defeatist group, younger and bolder in its cowardly undertakings, was to dominate more and more completely in the following years what remained of the patriotic elements in the Liberal party.

Among the Socialists also there were two conflicting currents: according to an oft-repeated saying, there were those who preferred death to slavery and there were those who thought that life is always worth living, even if in a concentration camp. The first group was represented by Léon Blum, and the second by Paul Faure. Today Léon Blum is in prison and Paul Faure has a seat in the national council founded by Marshal Pétain. In order to understand the significance of this split in the French Socialist Party, it is necessary to bear in mind the philosophy which has almost constantly predominated in this party from its beginning until its end in 1940. It was a rather vulgar materialism in which humanitarian sentimentality was bound up with a pronounced tendency towards low ethical standards. This philosophy was shared by both Blum and Paul Faure, but there was a considerable difference between these two men: in the group led by Paul Faure there was not any feeling by which the hedonistic spirit could be held in check. Forced to choose, they would unhesitatingly prefer slavery to death, for in slavery it is still possible to hope for gratifications which death most certainly brings to an end. They were men of peace at any price who would refuse to die for Danzig or for any other cause. Among Blum and his followers, on the contrary, the hedonistic tendency, while very strong, could be held in check, if a choice had to be made, by an idealistic heroism coming down from the French Revolution.* "Against an aggression of Nazi Ger-

* Let us pay tribute here to the young socialist, Léo Lagrange, a member of the first Blum Cabinet. After having upheld with great determination the policy of *death rather than servitude*, he was killed in action in June 1940. His character was described and the story of his death told by Jean Weiller in the *Commonweal* (Aug. 29, 1941, *The Death of a Frenchman*). It should be recalled, also, that the patriotic Socialists, headed by Blum, were, together with *six* Christian Democrats, the only deputies who stood in the opposition when the panic-stricken Parliament voted the Republic out of existence in behalf of the Nazi-sponsored government of Marshal Pétain.

many," Blum declared in 1936, "the French workmen will stand up as a single man." But Blum could not find either in his own character or in his past, the extraordinary energy which could alone have assured the triumph of the policy of national salvation over the enemies from without and from within. Confronted by the war, Blum reacted in a very patriotic way; but in 1936 his foreign policy showed all the irresolution and inconsistency which had characterized that of his predecessors and was to characterize that of his successors. He, also, made a contribution to the policy of appeasement.

The greatest factor of confusion in the foreign policy of the People's Front was the attitude of the Communist party. Its attitude in foreign affairs was as new, paradoxical and suspicious as it was in religious matters.

At the time the Communist party was founded (1920), two great countries were forcibly cut off from the rest of the European community, defeated Germany and Communist Russia. Between these two outlaws a collusion was unavoidable. This took place in 1922 with the Treaty of Rapallo which established rather close economic collaboration between the two countries. The system instituted at Rapallo lasted until 1934. But when the hold of Nazism became stronger in Germany and the old Prussian tradition of the *Drang nach Osten* was taken over by the Nazis, the restored power of Germany was felt as a threat in Moscow as well as in Paris. The Soviet government was led by circumstances to look for collaboration with France just as the Czars had done under similar circumstances. Abandoning its habitual attitude of insulting contempt towards the bourgeois democracies, the Moscow government joined the League of Nations as early as 1934, and signed pacts of mutual assistance with Czechoslovakia and with France the following year.

As soon as the Soviets relied upon the military force of France to hold the Nazi menace in check, it became impossible for their supporters in France to continue their systematic destruction of French power. Until then the foreign policy of the French Communist Party had been simply one of negation. In its fight against militarism and imperialism, the French Communist Party had constantly displayed a particular animosity towards the policy of the French government, no matter what it was, and no matter who the men in power. Openly anti-patriotic, the French Communists seemed to detest French patriotism more than any other patriotism. Completely submissive to the Russian leaders of the Third International, they were, for almost fifteen years, the most cynically anti-French element within the French community.

As early as the first months of 1934, the Soviet policy of rapprochement with France was accompanied by patriotic statements, at first discreetly, and then boldly, in the French Communist press. Within a few months the Communists had become the champions of the national dignity outraged by the Fascist powers. While their Parliamentary mouthpieces denounced, sometimes with remarkable clear-sightedness, the mortal danger represented by the policy of the Fascist states, their propaganda endeavored to stir up a revival of patriotism in the masses. The tricolor flag was hoisted alongside the red flag at popular demonstrations. The *Marseillaise* was sung between two stanzas of the *International*. Pictures of heroes of the French Revolution were put up beside those of Marx and Lenin. Everybody knew that all this was but the conscientious execution of an order from Moscow. But what would be the effect of this political attitude of the Communists, so far as the feelings of the masses were concerned? For a while it looked as though *revolutionary patriotism* was about to come to life again. The association of patriotic feeling with revolutionary feeling had made the French invincible many times. Was it again about to strike the tyrants with terror?

It terrified mostly the French conservatives, and we witnessed the resurgence in them of the spirit of the émigrés of 1792 who had allied themselves with the monarchs of Europe against patriotic and revolutionary France. But while in 1792 the émigrés were at Coblentz, on the other side of the frontier, in 1936, 1937 and 1938 we saw the new army of émigrés establish itself in the very heart of France,—in the press, in the literary world, in the public service, in the military forces, everywhere. It was a strange army, and the more redoubtable since it wore no uniform; composed of a mass of irresponsible people which a handful of clever men maneuvered with catchwords discreetly suggested or boldly proclaimed, as the case required. It was said that the Communists working for their Russian masters wanted to drag France into a war against Germany. It was thus suggested that the threats of war did not come from Germany but rather from Russia and . . . why not? . . . from France . . . from this France which had a People's Front government and a mutual assistance pact with the Soviets.

The opportunistic patriotism displayed by the

French Communists at the order of Moscow, and suddenly suppressed on the eve of the war at another order of Moscow, does not seem to have worked any profound change in the dispositions of the working masses. Yet it was an event of the first importance because of its repercussions on the parties of the Right and on the whole conservative and reactionary section of the nation, to which the task of defending the country was especially entrusted. As long as the Communists professed themselves anti-patriotic, as long as they played the role of relentless adversaries of every policy of national strength, the men of the Right could combine advantageously the honor of being the best defenders of order against Communism, and that of being the best defenders of France against Germany. But the day the Communists became the most ardent supporters of resistance to Nazi Germany, the French Right began to be won over by the idea that the real enemies of peace were not the Nazis, but those who wanted to oppose, if need be by the force of arms, the expansion of their tyranny. What a triumphal revenge! For many years, the French nationalist party had been accused of jeopardizing the interests of peace. It was now their turn to describe their adversaries as warmongers. Thanks to the existence of the

Franco-Soviet Pact and to the chauvinistic campaigns conducted by the French Communists, it was relatively easy to convince an important part of public opinion that the policy of resistance was nothing else but the enforcement of a plan engineered by the men of Moscow for the triumph of world revolution. Such was the anger of the French public against the Communists that any fantastic story had a good chance of being believed provided it seemed to throw a new light on the wickedness of the Communists. And so it was that the press opposing the People's Front began to repeat almost unanimously, and with an ever more striking docility, the catchphrases coined in the laboratories of the Nazi propaganda bureau.

VIII

Our Enemies' Enemies Are Our Friends

In the second chapter I attempted a description of the French Catholic bourgeoisie as it appeared to me in 1920, that is, right after the victory. A survey of the same social group in 1938, a short time before the defeat, reveals the bewildering changes which had come over French society during those eighteen years.

First of all, the limits of the group are much less clearcut, at least on one side. In 1920 the Catholic bourgeoisie was clearly distinct from another bourgeoisie, the anti-clerical bourgeoisie. The Catholic bourgeoisie, then, had its own newspapers

—and read no others—, its own doctors, its own druggists and its own lawyers. Alongside of it, and just as sure of itself and just as confident in its dogmas, the free-thinking bourgeoisie had its own lawyers, its doctors, its druggists and its newspapers. Between these two sections of the middle class there was as little intercourse as possible: marriages were rare, and social relations were ordinarily limited to those required by business. Eighteen years later the picture is altogether different: the anti-clerical bourgeoisie has lost faith in its dogmas, and is disturbed by what it believes, not without some reason, to be the consequences of an anti-clerical policy. The man whose grandfather, a mason of high degree, had championed the secular school, is so disquieted by the socialist and communist workingmen among the former pupils of that school, that he contributes to the support of the parish school and draws closer to Catholic circles. He feels the need of allying himself with the Catholic bourgeois against the common enemy: the revolutionary proletariat.[18] So far as foreign and

[18] It goes without saying that these dispositions of the bourgeoisie constituted a serious danger for Catholic institutions: they risked being exploited in behalf of class interests. I believe that on the whole they protected themselves fairly well. I have in mind a big Catholic school which lost a lot of money for having refused to forbid its professors of economics to teach theories considered "socialistic" by its trustees.

social politics are concerned, it is no longer possible to speak of the Catholic bourgeoisie; we must simply say *the bourgeoisie. Candide, Gringoire, Je Suis Partout, Le Matin, Le Jour* are read about equally by grandsons of the papal Zouaves and grandsons of the admirers of Garibaldi.

In the Catholic bourgeoisie of 1920 all political feeling was dominated by an aversion for Germany and for those who were suspected of weakening France before her ever powerful adversary. The Catholic bourgeoisie of 1920 was thoroughly anti-German. For it Germany was enemy number one. It had supported the atheist Clémenceau, it was fond of the free-thinker Poincaré, it was ready to uphold any government which would assert an uncompromising policy toward Germany. In 1938, hatred rages in the bourgeoisie. There had never been such hatred. The reading of each day's papers is a feast of hatred. But what do they hate? Is it still Germany? Few indeed are the bourgeois who still think that Germany is enemy number one. The object of their hatred is precisely the whole group of persons and things that Hitler himself hates with frenzy. This community of hates produces, in relation to Hitler Germany, irresolution in some people, unavowed sympathy in some others, open sympathy in some others, in a few, admiration. It becomes practically impossible to say where mischievous stupidity ends and where treason begins. Through a skillfully indirect method, propaganda has achieved the artillery preparation of which we spoke at the beginning of chapter six: the motorized columns can advance, Hitler has already won the battle of France.

It is by the same strategy that he hopes to win the battle of the world. He knows very well that none of his conquests, beginning with that of the German people, will be firmly secure as long as he has not succeeded in producing among the people of the Western Hemisphere the same irresolution, the same sympathy, and the same treason as in France. Whoever has observed the technique used in France, and observes what is now happening in certain countries of the New World is struck by the identity of the method the aggressor follows for the conquest, at first unnoticeable, of reputedly impregnable strongholds. It is a psychological device extremely simple in its principle and infinitely varied in its applications:

You will learn first to hate what I hate and those whom I hate; my enemies will be your enemies and you will have no enemies except my enemies. Then one day you will raise your eyes toward me to implore my protection against the common enemy, and I will come to you as your master: but if you resist, it will be too late and your strength will abandon you.

Who were these enemies the French had to learn to hate so that their will to resist Fascist and Nazi aggression could be destroyed? Who were these common enemies the hatred of whom was to establish a kind of solidarity, a kind of connivance, a kind of friendship between Hitler and his allies on the one hand, and many Frenchmen on the other? Here I would call attention to a point of capital importance: if Hitler and his allies had simply incited the French to hate, in union with them, honest people and very good institutions, they would have displayed a disastrous psychological naïveté. Their policy would only have won the support of scoundrels. Now, they needed both the support of scoundrels and the connivance of "decent people." For scoundrels can do little unless they are aided by "decent people." To win the help of the scoundrels they would exploit the hatred of the just and the weak; to win the connivance of the decent people (or those who are reputed to be such and wish to preserve their reputation), they would direct the forces of hatred against really criminal persons and really detestable things. It is impossible to understand anything of the psychological strategy employed by the international Fascists and Nazis unless this method of confusion is constantly borne in mind:

> *In order that you become more certainly my accomplice, by becoming the blind enemy of my enemies, I will teach you to hate indiscriminately and with the same fervor the just and the criminal; a day will come when you will no longer be able to distinguish between good and evil, and in your perverted conscience you will no longer find the strength to fight and to die; then I will come to you.*

Let us imagine an average French bourgeois who eats his breakfast and relishes the quarter of an hour of delightful hating that his daily paper supplies him with every day. What is he taught to hate? Nothing is more enlightening than a consideration of the objects delivered to his hatred.

The Jews have the first place. During the years preceding the war, anti-semitic feeling increased tremendously in the French bourgeoisie, and the infamous racial decrees issued by the Pétain government caused no surprise to those aware of the situation. In this connection it is very interesting to compare what happened in Italy with what happened in France. In both cases the anti-semitic measures were imposed by the Nazi conqueror. But it was said that in Italy the anti-semitic policy was considered revolting by ninety-five persons out of a hundred. In France, on the contrary, while it is probable that the people almost unanimously condemned it as stupid and perverse, it is certain that an important section of the bourgeoisie (the truest supporters of Marshal Pétain) welcomed it with delight and saw in it the reward of persevering efforts. Why was there so little anti-semitism in Italy? Above all because there are very few Jews on Italian soil. As to the anti-semitism of the French bourgeoisie, I do not think that it should be related to any particular cause; it is sufficiently accounted for by the general features of anti-semitic psychology: jealousy of business men, resentment of doctors without patients and of lawyers without cases, pharisaism of bad Christians who like to throw on the Jews the whole blame for the death of Our Lord (thus relieving themselves from the disturbing thought that it is *our* sins which caused the death of Jesus on the Cross), etc. The Dreyfus case had shown that in time of crisis it was possible to inflame this anti-semitism into a murderous passion. The state of confusion and uncertainty of the last prewar years facilitated the accomplishment of this criminal work. In the presence of a confused situation, when great misfortunes occur without anyone knowing whence they come, stupidity, fear and wickedness find a particular satisfaction in imagining that all the trouble comes from a clearly defined group, plotting in the dark—from an occult force mysteriously unified and conscious, intelligent and secret as the devil himself. A whole book could be written on the psychology of the belief in the occult groups which are assigned the role of explaining public misfortunes to the simple-minded. In France, within the space of a few generations, we had the non-juring priests, the Jesuits, the Freemasons, the "strong arm of Germany," the Intelligence Service, the Maffia (1934-35), and finally the Jews. These collective beliefs can well drive people to murder unless they are held in check by opposite and stronger collective beliefs. Now the only force in France which could hold in check the anti-semitic passion was the spirit of equal justice for all which the French Revolution, in spite of its own crimes, has blown upon the world. At the beginning of the XXth century the spirit of the French Revolution had still enough life to obtain, at the cost of an epic struggle, justice for the Jew Dreyfus; but in 1938 the French Revolution, as we have seen, had been a thing of the past for twenty years. Some Catholic forces asserted themselves with great nobility against the ever-growing anti-semitism.[19] Their interventions were of help to many souls, but so far as immediate temporal results were concerned, these apostles of unadulterated Christianity, when confronted by *L'Action Française*, *Je Suis Partout*, etc., were in a position similar to that of the Greek army before the motorized Nazi divisions. Owing to the presence of several Jews in the Blum cabinet, it was easy to direct against the Jews the anger stirred up by the policy of the People's Front and to launch the slogan *France in the hands of the Jews.*

France in the hands of the Jews! Was not this the supreme evil? But if it was the supreme evil, the enslavement of France by these Nazis, who knew so well how to fight and revile and torture the Jews, was but a lesser evil in the eyes of certain French "nationalists." Hitler had already won the battle of France.

After the Jews, the Freemasons, an ambiguous

---

[19] Let us mention in particular the admirable writings of Jacques Maritain. See: *A Christian Looks at the Jewish Question* (Longmans) and *Ransoming the Time*, Chapters VI and VII (Scribner).

and fluid kind of people, against whom the French had well-founded grievances. Here the weapon of confusion triumphed because French Freemasonry, an essentially bourgeois society, had in the preceding years suffered the same disintegration as the liberal bourgeoisie of which it was an offspring. Few masons remained faithful to the stupid and harmful dogmas which they had until recently spread so assiduously among the French (anti-religious ethics, individualism, belief in the inevitability of progress, etc.). In the general helter-skelter of the last years most masons took refuge in an opportunism in which ideology no longer played a role. A well-known Freemason, a veteran of anti-clerical struggles, Camille Chautemps, pronounced the famous phrase *We Liberals are no longer anti-clericals*. It is he who, as head of a People's Front government, organized the triumphal reception of Cardinal Pacelli in 1937; after that he received, according to diplomatic custom and without any apparent embarrassment, the highest papal decorations; a member of the first Pétain cabinet, he contributed to the capitulation. Today, he is in Washington; it would be interesting to know what he is doing there.

The adventures of M. Camille Chautemps illustrate perfectly the policy followed by most

Freemasons in recent years: they were ready to take any course, now allied with the Communists, now warming up to the Catholics; more mysterious than ever, they were more easily than ever cast in the role of the occult force which accounts for public misfortunes. To explain any political disaster, the ghost of Freemasonry could be successfully conjured up, for Freemasons had no longer any policy and followed every policy.

The Communists had been talked about so much and the French public felt so much anger and disgust about them that it was, in a way, both superfluous and boring to criticize them. Yet, if cleverly exploited, anti-communism could still furnish an invaluable theme of propaganda. It is easy to set forth the rules for a clever exploitation of the anti-communist motif:

First rule: insist on the idea that Communism is enemy number one, the supreme evil.[20]

Second rule: show that the Communists are at work wherever any great disaster occurs, and that they are the cause of all the trouble.

We have already seen, with regard to the Jews, how the first rule works. Fools and cowards are

[20] The Jews have already played the role of supreme evil. Can there be more than one supreme evil? Of course, for propaganda and for the public to which it is addressed, logic has no importance whatsoever.

easily convinced that what is not the greatest evil is a tolerable lesser evil. It is as though a hesitating traveller were told that if he takes the road to the left, he will find himself facing a machine gun; on the other hand, if he takes the road to the right, he will find himself facing a sub-machine gun. A machine gun is much more dangerous than a sub-machine gun: the sub-machine gun, therefore, is the lesser evil. The traveller still hesitates. So they drill into his head terrifying stories about the horrors of the machine gun; they talk so much about the machine gun that he forgets about the sub-machine gun. Then, as his resistance weakens, he is brow-beaten into making a choice. They convince him that he cannot remain forever at the crossroads. So he throws himself unarmed before the sub-machine gun, falls, riddled with bullets, and the wily advisers call it a day. Such is the story of the German conservatives. Such is the story of the French conservatives. All conservatives still remaining in the world, please note.

Herr Thyssen was a great German industrialist, a conservative and a Catholic. He supported Hitler and the rising Nazi movement with the resources of his immense fortune. Why did he act this way? Since Herr Thyssen showed later that he was capable of an honest and even courageous attitude, it can be assumed that his generosity to Hitler was due more to stupidity than to wickedness. Apparently someone convinced him that Germany had to choose between Communism and Nazism, and that the lesser evil should be chosen. But Herr Thyssen—to his honor—proved unwilling to follow the road of crime to the end. He opposed the war, sought refuge in France and denounced the Nazis. When victorious, the Nazis put him in a concentration camp. Such is the logical development of the policy of the lesser evil.

The second rule was brilliantly successful in a variety of applications. Thanks to it, all the friends of France were held up to the French public as Communists, or as allies of the Communist cause, or as people whose policies accorded with that of the Communists. Finally, it became possible to suggest to the French that France itself had become the accomplice of Communism, and that she was not worth the trouble of defending against the only power capable of holding Communism in check, Hitler Germany. Here are a few examples.

When the Japanese bombers massacred the population of Shanghai, *Gringoire* would have its readers believe that the real capital of China was Moscow. As a matter of fact, the government of

Chiang Kai-shek had crushed Communism in China. But who cares about the truth? Japan, the defender of civilization against Communism: this was another smoke-screen behind which the enemies of France could advance with the French "nationalists" unconcerned about stopping them.

We have shown in another chapter the important role played by the Ethiopian war in the disorganization of French patriotism. The Ethiopian war was really the beginning of the World War, and this first battle found the French nationalists on the side of the enemies of France. The war in China was—and is today more than ever—another great battle in the world struggle. The following incident shows how even a remote conflict was exploited in France in favor of the enemy. During the winter 1937-1938, a Catholic association for the study of racial and missionary problems asked me to preside at a discussion on China. The speakers were a priest who had just returned from an extensive trip through China, and a Chinese college girl. Such was the terroristic pressure exercised by the international Fascist party on the French Catholics that I almost had to apologize for my presence at this meeting. Expressing a feeling of justice and pity toward China while she was being tortured was to risk displeasing . . .

not the Japanese embassy (which, I am sure, was perfectly indifferent) but ... the friends which Japan, the aggressor, had in Europe, and the friends that the friends of Japan had in France. The coalition of murderers formed a large range embracing the whole world, and this international gang of bandits maintained patrols everywhere. Nothing was insignificant in the eyes of these scouts. In order to avoid embarrassment to the respected institution in which I was teaching, I asked the organizers of the discussion not to mention my academic connections. I am not exaggerating: a Catholic university could very easily find itself in trouble for the simple reason that one of its professors was accused of speaking out against Japanese aggression. Were not the Chinese Communists? After having declared that I was speaking only as a French citizen, I explained frankly the meaning of what was happening around us. And addressing certain Frenchmen, the self-appointed "defenders of the West," "defenders of the Latin order," who had played so consistently the game of France's enemies, I exclaimed: "Your cause is now triumphing and international disputes will no longer be settled by assemblies of jurists, but on the fields of battle and amidst the ruins of cities: yesterday Ethiopia, today China, tomorrow France."

But the event which best lent itself to the exploitation of the Communist danger in behalf of the enemies of France was the Spanish civil war. Let us recall the rule of propaganda stated above: *In order that you become more certainly my accomplice, by becoming the blind enemy of my enemies, I will teach you to hate indiscriminately and with the same fervor the just and the criminal; a day will come when you will no longer be able to distinguish between good and evil.* . . . As a matter of fact, the campaigns of moral corruption waged among the French in connection with the wars in Ethiopia and in China were unleashed under difficult conditions. You could hardly expect the French to hate the Ethiopians, even by telling them terrifying stories about slavery and judicial barbarism in Ethiopia,—or to hate the Chinese on the pretence that they were Communists. You could at best direct their hatred against the English: but after all, the case against the English reduced itself to the fact that they were not indifferent to their economic and strategic interests in Ethiopia and China. The Japanese, on the contrary, could be blamed for their savage bombings, and the Italians for their clouds of mustard gas. In the case of Ethiopia and that of China no honest man could fail to know who were the criminals. In spite of these unfavorable conditions, the psychological offensives undertaken in regard to the Chinese and especially the Ethiopian wars succeeded brilliantly. It was thus established that many people who were believed honest were not, and that there was an enormous number of fools ready to be taken in by the crudest liars.

But the Spanish war was an altogether different case. What a godsend for the enemies of France was this thirty months slaughter in which one million three hundred thousand persons lost their lives! What a godsend for the enemies of France were the killings of priests, the desecrations of churches which stirred up, in France as elsewhere, so much anger against the Spanish Reds! How the enemies of France must have cheered, each time a new outrage or a new sacrilege was committed by the adversaries of Spanish Fascism! After having seen service under rather unfavorable conditions, the principle *our enemies' enemies are our friends*, could function under ideal conditions. For after all, the armies of Fascist Italy and Nazi Germany in Spain were not fighting poor Chinese peasants nor poor Ethiopian peasants, who, as everybody knew, had never tried to invade Italy or Japan. They were fighting the Communists of Castile and the anarchists of Catalonia, supported and controlled by the men of Moscow; they were fighting the priest-killers and the incendiaries of churches; they were fighting the Republican government, guilty of many weaknesses; they were fighting those who wanted to destroy Christian faith in Spain.[21] What an incredible piece of luck for the Fascists and Nazis! On the side of their enemies there were—at last!—a great number of unquestionable criminals whom every honest man had to consider as enemies. The consequence was that not only liars or fools, as in the Ethiopian war, but also really virtuous men, favored the victory of the Fascist and Nazi armies. Innumerable Frenchmen,—and not only rascals and idiots, as during the Ethiopian conflict—supported in their speeches and in their hearts the armies of Mussolini and Hitler. The solidarity thus established was to be confirmed every day for two and a half years by the daily news from Spain.

I intend to refrain from any judgment on what was, or what might have been, French policy toward the Spanish tragedy. I simply point out

[21] They were also fighting the Catholics of the Basque country. But it was easy not to say anything about this side of the conflict, or better, to tell people that the Basques were "Christian Reds," more detestable than the Communists.

the importance of this psychological fact: for a long, painful and heartbreaking period which came to an end only a few months before the official outbreak of the World War, innumerable Frenchmen, possibly the majority, were morally at the side of Hitler and his allies in a struggle to which everybody ascribed a decisive importance. Was it psychologically possible for these millions of Frenchmen, in a few months after the (official) conclusion of hostilities, to turn as one man on Hitler and his allies, and fight them with unwavering resolution? It was much to hope for.

During the first months of the Spanish war, a plane of the Republican air-force dropped its bombs (probably by mistake) on a German warship. In retaliation, the German fleet bombarded severely the city of Almeria. Gustave Hervé commented on this event in an article entitled "Hurrah for the Germans!" But we must recall who this Gustave Hervé is. Thirty years ago he was one of the most notorious members of the Socialist party. He was currently called *the man who dragged the flag in the dung*. He had, as a matter of fact, been convicted in court for an article in which he said that, in certain circumstances, the flag of "imperialism" (but there is no flag in France other than the French flag) should be dragged in the dung rather than be hoisted to the place of honor. He represented the most anti-militaristic wing of Socialism and edited a paper called *La Guerre Sociale* (The Social War). In 1914 Hervé quickly became an advocate of the most militant patriotism, and changed the name of his paper to *La Victoire*. On the morrow of the War Hervé was still socialist and advocated a patriotic socialism. But in the following years, his political conversion made great progress, and soon he was nothing more than an ordinary Rightist, whose chief originality was to have, in other days, dragged the flag in the dung. His paper had become one of those curious sheets—and there were quite a few in France in recent years—which survived in spite of a very small circulation (I do not recall having seen a copy of *La Victoire* in a number of years). These curious sheets with few subscribers and no sale at newsstands played nonetheless a considerable role in the formation of public opinion, for their editorials were cited every day in the reviews of the press given by the big newspapers and radio newscasts.

Once his political conversion was complete, Gustave Hervé became the advocate of the *Authoritarian Republic*, a form of dictatorial state over which he wanted Marshal Pétain to preside.

On the other hand, Hervé was one of the first to recommend a rapprochement between France and Hitler Germany.

Hurrah for the Germans! . . . who would have believed it twenty years earlier, when *La Victoire* was one of the favorite papers of the nationalist groups, then so relentlessly anti-German! Soon the Germans would be in Paris and Marshal Pétain become the head of an authoritarian state which was not even granted the honor of calling itself a republic. The military occupation of Paris caused the suspension of all newspapers for a few days. Then one morning three newspapers were permitted to appear. *La Victoire* of Gustave Hervé was one of the three. In the short space of time which elapsed between the cheer Hervé gave to the Nazis in connection with the bombardment of Almeria and the welcome he did not fail to give them when they entered into Paris, Marshal Pétain had made the acquaintance of the new German army. As ambassador of the French Republic at Madrid, he had attended the triumphal parade of those Nazi aviators, who were by then perfectly trained and ready to make a shamble of the cities of Poland and France a few months later. All these events betray a terrible logic. Long before war was declared, Hitler had won the battle of France.

Just after the Munich agreement (1938), Thierry Maulnier wrote that in the war which had just been avoided, the defeat of Germany would have meant "the collapse of the authoritarian regimes which constitute the main rampart against the Communist revolution," and that the victory of France "would have been less a French victory than the victory of the principles which are rightly considered to lead to the ruin of France and of civilization." Thus, in the case of a German victory, there would have been only partial evil: only France would have been destroyed. On the contrary, a French victory would have involved the ruin of France and that of civilization. And who was Thierry Maulnier?—a brilliant and talented young writer who had won a leading position among Fascist intellectuals.

In spite of all we have said about the evolution of French nationalism—identical observations could be made apropos of several other nationalisms—the reader may be astonished that a young man could with no apparent danger of having his neck broken dare to tell the French public, recently so proud, that the victory of France would have been more to be feared than that of Germany. To give a pretence of decency to such a cynical confession, he had to have an overwhelmingly convincing argument: this argument was supplied by the mutual assistance pact between France and Soviet Russia.

We have already alluded to this pact which played such a considerable role in the psychological preparation of the war. Did this pact mean, as the Nazi propagandists and their French collaborators wanted to make the world believe, a collusion of French revolutionary forces with the revolutionary colossus of the East? This interpretation might have had some appearance of truth if the Franco-Soviet pact had been concluded during the regime of the People's Front. But it was negotiated and signed before the People's Front came into power, and by men of the Right, the patriot Barthou and the adventurer Laval. It is also fitting to recall that during the long period when Germany, governed most of the time by the Catholic Center, maintained friendly relations with Soviet Russia, nobody ever accused her of favoring the world revolution. Except for the Communists, all Frenchmen abhorred the thought that a victory over the enemies of France could be at the same time a victory for Soviet Russia. The whole question was whether, in order to save peace against the Nazi menace, it was indispensable to arrange for the cooperation of the French and the Russian armies. To this question some French patriots well known for their conservative ideas, and some military chiefs, replied affirmatively. They were perfectly aware of the risk involved in a promise of mutual assistance between France and the Soviets: they decided it was necessary to run the risk. Four years later Mr. Chamberlain and Lord Halifax came to be of the same opinion and made desperate efforts to conclude an alliance with Russia. It was too late. In the meantime the Fascist and Nazi bloc had conquered Ethiopia, Austria, Czechoslovakia, Spain and Albania; the Russians had lost all confidence in the resolution and reliability of the powers which had tolerated or facilitated these conquests. They decided to come to an understanding with the Nazis, and the Nazis showed themselves delighted to come to an agreement with them.

Tragic situations are those which do not admit of any simple solution. France, in 1938, was in the throes of a tragedy which only a pure and strong heroism could master. But French nationalists readily assumed the task of simplifying the situation. The salvation of France demanded both an uncompromising fight against the Communist party and military cooperation with the Moscow heads of the same party. This was the really tragic aspect of the French position. The French conservatives who had initiated the Franco-Soviet pact understood this well. At the time the pact was negotiated (1934-1935), the conservative public had displayed a rather remarkable comprehension of the situation. There was much talk then of that French king who made an alliance with the Great Turk without the slightest thought of becoming a Mussulman, and of that Cardinal, minister of another king of France, who allied himself with the Protestant princes of Germany while he was crushing the political power of the French Protestants. Without weighing very carefully the value of these analogies, people concluded patriotically that they had to meet the moral difficulties of this two-fold duty: to collaborate with the Soviet Union in order to prevent war, and to fight the Third International whose links with the Soviet government were known to everybody.

As a matter of fact this frame of mind was still possible in 1934 and 1935 before the Ethiopian war, the People's Front and the Spanish war. But in 1938, after two years of People's Front's administration and of Spanish war, the French nationalist world was too corrupted by fear and hatred to endure any longer the torments of such a tragedy within everyone's conscience. Henceforth they would no longer say *We are against Communism*, *but for France and, if we must, at the price of an agreement with Russia!* Henceforth they would simply say *We are against Communism, against the People's Front, we stand with the enemies of the Soviet Union!*

Soon all was ready for the conquest of the Bohemian stronghold by the Nazis. France had an alliance with Czechoslovakia and the Czechs were the most faithful of her allies. They had an excellent army, powerful fortifications and first-class equipment. The geographical location of Czechoslovakia plus the quality of its army, made this little state a formidable adversary for Germany. What argument could be used to blind the French to the shamefulness of the perjury expected of France by her enemies? What argument could blind them to the imminent danger of war and defeat which would result for France from a new surrender in Central Europe? The crushing argument was simple and easy, and gave cowardice the aspect of virtue. This argument, which had already worked so many times against France without apparently losing any of its force, was that of the Communist danger.

Not that the Czechs were Communists. But the opinion prevailed, and no doubt it was well founded, that France could not give any effective aid to Czechoslovakia without engaging in close cooperation with Russia. It was a matter of geographical determinism. France could not honor her commitments and preserve her national existence without implementing her accord with the Communist giant and accepting all the risks of such an accord. The principle *our enemies' enemies are our friends* was—at last—to work directly against France. For if France was to have a really French policy by showing herself true to her promises and aware of the requirements of her own salvation, certain Frenchmen, the majority of those who called themselves nationalists, the Frenchmen whom history especially entrusted with the duty of assuring national defence, would consider that she had joined the camp of the enemy. Hitler had already won the battle of France and young Thierry Maulnier could, without risking his neck, reveal the moral of the story.[22]

---

[22] Let us pay tribute to the nationalist minority which remained patriotic to the very end. The soul of the group was Henri de Kerillis, a conservative, who became, in the last few years, the object of the fierce hatred of the conservatives. He was, if I remember correctly, the only Rightist deputy who voted against the Munich agreement. A determined enemy of socialism, he did not hesitate to acknowledge a certain patriotic attitude of Léon Blum and to exclaim in the Chamber: "M. Blum, you are a great Frenchman." He was the friend of Paul Reynaud. Blum and Reynaud are now in prison. It is very fortunate that de Kerillis was able to reach the United States.

When war was about to break out in September, 1938, the condition of French and British forces was certainly very poor. If the defenders of the Munich agreement had contented themselves with claiming that France, because of the irreparable faults of the past, found herself physically compelled to surrender her most faithful ally, they would still deserve the charge of having nourished fantastic illusions, and of having deceived the French people. For there was not the slightest chance that the Nazis would give France and Great Britain the time to compensate and more than compensate for the loss of the Czech army, the Czech fortifications, the Czech airforce, not to mention a loss of prestige big with incalculable consequences. But the men of Munich and their supporters did not think it necessary to apologize for having imposed on France the most disgraceful capitulation in her history. They went so far as to maintain that nothing shameful had taken place. They went so far as to maintain that there had not been any surrender. Like Hitler and Mussolini, Daladier was given a triumphal welcome on his return to his capital. It can be said that the popular demonstrations that greeted him when he came back from the meeting in which the destiny of France was sealed, had been engineered years in advance by the infamous press we have had so many occasions to mention. Wise observers did not fail to remark that such a lack of common sense on the part of the people of Paris was a still more disturbing symptom than the folly of a government. During the following months, we came to realize that a number of persons whose common sense should have been protected by their social position, their moral character and their education, did not think any more soundly than the average reader of a corrupt press. A few days after Munich, I wrote to the rector of a French University a letter which was, as might be expected, extremely sad. In his reply he censured my pessimism rather contemptuously, and to reassure me, stressed the fact that the Daladier government had won a complete victory over . . . the labor movement, by crushing an attempted general strike. If my letter was so sad, it was evidently because it had been written before the defeat of the labor unions was certain. Once more, the danger of a social crisis acted as a smoke-screen behind which the enemy could advance unhampered. Of these two events, the betrayal at Munich and the failure of the general strike, was not the second the more important? Now, this was an event worth rejoicing over. "The

September crisis," concluded the rector, "has cleared the atmosphere."

Such was the degree of idiocy reached by a man of high education and great virtue. I attach even more significance to the declaration made some time later by a Bishop well known for his strength of character and nobility of spirit. During the first World War he had fulfilled with a magnificent dignity his duty as the spiritual head of a battered city. Throughout his long career, he had always been extremely careful to warn Catholics against anything which might endanger the purity of their patriotism. In spite of his sense of justice and his great charity, he had a strong anti-German feeling, and I think he was one of those who never believed in the disarmament of Germany or in the peaceable dispositions of German democracy. As late as 1932 he severely criticized anybody who thought that France should no longer claim war reparations. In March 1938, he criticized indignantly the conduct of Cardinal Innitzer, Archbishop of Vienna, who welcomed the invaders of his country with the cry of *Heil Hitler!* But in June, 1938, I noticed a change in his reactions: he was thinking of a German expansion *eastward* as a lesser evil (*eastward*, that is into Russia, but to move an army from Germany into Russia, is it not necessary to trample on the body of Poland?). In December, 1938, in his pastoral letter for the new year, he congratulated the French government for having adopted at Munich a solution which, considering the faults of the past, he called that of justice, honor and peace.

Before being conquered on the battlefield, France was defeated from within. This defeat from within, which made possible her defeat on the battlefield, is to be understood in relation to the general characteristics of the totalitarian state.

IX

What Is a Traitor?

ACCORDING to the best students of political science, the totalitarian regime comes into existence the moment a *gang of armed men* declare that they are the State.[23] This gang is the vanguard of a party and owes to the support of the party the strength that enables it to take command of the administration. The party itself, although a political minority, enjoys enormous power of expansion on the grounds of its *ideology*. This ideology is simple,

[23] Cf. Waldemar Gurian, *Future of Bolshevism*, Sheed and Ward, New York, 1936, and Elie Halévy, *L'ère des tyrannies*, Gallimard, Paris, 1938. I wish to express my thanks to the *Review of Politics*, Notre Dame, Indiana, for giving me permission to reproduce here a part of an article published in its June issue of 1941: *The European Crisis and the Downfall of the French Republic*.

WHAT IS A TRAITOR?

primitive, brutal, and of such a nature as to appeal to the lowest instincts under a mask of grandeur.

These are the three elements of the totalitarian regime: a gang (with a gang leader), a party and an ideology. The core of the system lies in the identification of the party with the whole of the State.

The consequences of this identification are plain. Whereas the State is confined within certain territorial boundaries, the influence of the party, propagated by its ideology, goes far beyond the State boundaries. It pervades all the space open to it. There is nothing in it to prevent it from pervading the whole world. Thus, the totalitarian State becomes the head of an international community which divides its followers in other countries from their own national allegiances.

According to traditional concepts, the allegiance of the citizen to his State or country is one and indivisible. The citizen owes allegiance to his country alone. He does not owe allegiance to any temporal community outside of his State or country.[24]

[24] The idea of a League of Nations, although it implied the acknowledgment of a temporal unity superior to the nation, in no way implied that the political allegiance of the citizen should be divided. Since the League of Nations is a society made up of national units, it presupposes the allegiance of the citizen to his nation and can not conflict with it. The influence of the League of Nations can not affect the citizen without passing through the

These traditional concepts were to be severely tried by the great politico-social transformations of the twentieth century. The Workingmen's International Association offers a striking example of a temporal organization capable of provoking occasionally a conflict of allegiance within the State. As we have already remarked, the leaders of several European countries had reason to fear on the eve of the war of 1914 that the socialist workingmen, on mobilization day, would follow the tendency to revolutionary secession rather than the tendency to national integration. In 1914, however, the risk of national unity splitting under the pressure of the international proletariat did not materialize.

After the First World War the danger of a conflict of allegiance within the States took a new and more dreadful form. Whereas before 1914 the Workingmen's International Association had no steady connection with any particular government, the Third International, founded in Moscow in 1919, was practically identified with the Soviet government. Consequently, every member of the International abroad was a potential agent of the Russian Soviet State in its expansionist enterprises.

State, in such a way that the unity of the State and its authority over its members remains unimpaired and thoroughly respected.

WHAT IS A TRAITOR?

The danger was felt intensely in the countries neighboring on the Soviet Union.

In fact, the Soviet Union did not achieve any territorial aggrandizement, at least in Europe, until the coveted territories were surrendered to it by the Nazis (Pact of August, 1939). So long as the European order was not completely destroyed by Nazi Germany, the Russian State, although it had agents everywhere through its identification with the Communist International, did not succeed in repairing any of the huge losses it had undergone between 1917 and 1919. Among the reasons for that failure, let us emphasize the very character of the Third International as a strongly organized community plainly linked to a government. The Third International was easily recognizable wherever it was active. In every city of every country, its office-addresses were as familiar as those of any bank or school. It had its newspapers, its bulletins, and posters, etc. Nobody could join it, even as a mere sympathizer, without being aware of what he was doing. The Third International could not enjoy the advantage of those obscure adherences that are given, in the darkness of uncertain consciences, to less conspicuously organized communities. On the other hand, since the Third International was obviously an instrument of the Soviet Government, no patriot outside Russia could even think of joining it. This is the decisive point: if a country was betrayed in favor of Soviet expansion by some of its citizens, these citizens had the reputation of being bad citizens. Their case was comparatively clear, and comparatively easy to deal with.

In this connection the story of the meeting held at Tours in 1920 by the French Socialists assumes a symbolical meaning. The question was whether the French Socialist party should join the Third International. Everything seemed ready for a general adherence when a telegram from Moscow, signed Zinoviev (the famous *Zinoviev bomb*) warned the French that they would have to obey blindly the orders of Moscow. Then, those who were unwilling to be governed from abroad seceded. Their secession was a fatal blow to the influence of the Communist International in France. The Zinoviev bomb, by destroying the unity of the revolutionary proletariat, reduced to almost nothing the chances of a proletarian revolution.

Apparently Zinoviev did not know how to use a smokescreen. But Hitler knew. From the time he came to power in 1933 until June, 1940, he marched on Paris under the cover of a smokescreen. He has not yet given up the project of

WHAT IS A TRAITOR?

spreading the same smokescreen over the New World.

The international community of which Hitler was the head was not an openly organized community like the Communist International; it was not, like the Communist International, a community openly headed and subsidized from abroad. It was a subtle and fluid body whose activity was often inconspicuous, whose real aims were unknown to many of its members and whose limits were vague. In walking through French cities, you inevitably found a building bearing a sign in large letters: *Communist Party*, and you knew what was going on behind the sign. But you never saw anywhere a sign: *International Nazi Party*, *General Committee*, *Hitler*, *Goering*, *Hess*, etc. You became a member of the community headed by Hitler without registering at any office and without paying any fee. You could adhere to this community without necessarily knowing what you were doing. You could be a member of this community to a greater or lesser degree. You never knew exactly who belonged to it. It was a matter of inner choice more often decided in the darkness of an uncertain conscience than in the clear light of a criminal conscience. Adherence to the community of the international Nazis admitted of an unlimited number of degrees, and the adherents in the lower degrees were not less useful to the common cause than those whose adherence was unqualified and given with a complete awareness of its consequences. In this infernal house there were many mansions. There were some for traitors bought by the enemy, there were some for traitors moved by ambition, there were some for traitors moved by ideological passions, there were some for sympathizers of every degree, for the irresolute of every degree . . . the base of the pyramid was lost in the masses. It was therefore an extraordinarily solid base.

Was France betrayed? Maritain has given a very exact answer to this question in these words: "The impression that we all had here, that France had been betrayed on all sides squares doubtless with reality, provided only that in the word 'betrayal' we see something much broader, complex, something at once more tragic and less suggestive of criminal intent than is usually meant by the word."[25]

The image which the word traitor ordinarily brings to mind is that of an individual who, for the sake of money, performs services manifestly and consciously harmful to his country, such as espio-

[25] *France My Country*, Longmans, New York, 1941, p. 3.

nage and sabotage. If the word traitor is so understood, to the question: *was France betrayed?* we must certainly answer in the affirmative. But we must hasten to add that there have been traitors in all wars, at all times and in all countries, and that the cases of manifest treason,—I mean those cases in which money makes the treason manifest—are relatively easy to deal with. Law provides effective protection against treason for money; in peacetime, fines, prison, hard labor; in wartime, the death penalty.

After the political traitor comes the fanatic who receives orders from abroad and carries them out, not for money, but to satisfy a passion. Such was no doubt the case of most of the French Communist leaders. The French Communist Party, always submissive to the orders of Moscow, stopped the campaign of resistance to Nazi Germany as soon as the latter made a pact with Moscow. It tried to sabotage the mobilization. Once Poland was crushed, it recommended the immediate conclusion of peace on Hitler's terms. This policy of the Communist Party prompted relatively few prominent members of the Communist Party to resign. Everybody concluded that Communists were traitors—it was already a current opinion. Did it mean that they were paid to behave as they did? The great majority of the Communists who betrayed their country certainly never received a cent for their treason. There was no need to pay them. Money is not the only motive for treason.

The Communists received orders from abroad and carried them out. Others served the cause of the enemy without anybody giving them orders. Here confusion begins and the public does not know by what name to call these people. I am thinking of some famous writers who as early as 1936 or 1937 travelled through Germany and witnessed the great demonstrations of the Nazi Party, then told the French public in glowing terms of the wonderful things they had been shown. They explained that the Nazis were much more congenial than the French statesmen, that they had nothing against France, that they were effectively protecting Europe and culture against Communist barbarism, etc.[26] Were these propagandists bought? I am very much inclined to believe that they were not. There was no more need to pay them than there was to pay the fanatics of the Communist Party. They worked for an ideal—a wicked and stupid ideal. But is a country less effectively betrayed

[26] The most notorious of these propagandists was the novelist, Alphonse de Chateaubriant. Today he is carrying on his dirty work in occupied Paris.

when it is betrayed for an ideal rather than for money? I affirm that it is more effectively betrayed, for intellectual and moral corruption can achieve many things which ordinary corruption by money cannot achieve. Can you imagine a paid adventurer carrying on anti-French propaganda in the French Academy? Yet it was said that a certain member of the French Academy, notorious for his trips to Germany, greeted his colleagues with: *Long live Hitler, down with the Soviets!* Was he aware of his treason? This is not our concern. Shall we say that he was a traitor? He most assuredly was, and one of the most dangerous kind.

There were many traitors of this kind in the last years of the French Republic. What did they have to fear? There are laws to take care of the spy who sells a document of no value. There is no law against a member of the Academy who teaches the French in peacetime to shout: *Long live Hitler!* Society can only protect itself against traitors of this kind by extra-legal sanctions: dishonor, boycott, jeers, and beatings.

Apparently these benevolent propagandists for the enemy did not receive many beatings. Just as some robbers get protection from friends who themselves do not steal, so these French Hitlerites, when they were threatened by some kind of punishment, hid themselves in a crowd of conniving people who, though they did not like the Nazis, liked their friends and detested their enemies. And what about those who made up this crowd? Shall we call them traitors, too? It can not be denied that in their own way they helped to betray France.

A few recollections:

1933. The first group of Jewish refugees hunted out by the Nazis has just arrived in Paris. Cardinal Verdier, who never missed a chance to show his kindness, has expressed, in a few simple words, the hope that these outlaws would receive true hospitality. A few days later, I meet a young man belonging to the *Action Française*; he is indignant about the statement of Cardinal Verdier. For, of course, he hates the Jews. Like Hitler. With Hitler.

1935. A young and very distinguished philosopher explains to me the Ethiopian conflict. England has no need to worry about her lifeline to India. Nobody threatens it. On the desk of this defender of the West there is a royalist paper (not the *Action Française*, for he observes the letter of the condemnation). I open the paper and express my displeasure at seeing in it the name of a certain member of the Academy. "He is quite good on foreign policy." I read the article: it is a cynical exaltation of the Fascist aggression. The name of the author?

WHAT IS A TRAITOR?

The man who greeted his friends with *Long live Hitler*, etc.

1936. Lunch with the same philosopher. I am about to leave for Austria and I have just spent two hours at the German consulate to obtain my transit visa. A technicality prevented me from obtaining it. So I shall go via Switzerland. I say: "After passing two hours in front of Hitler's portrait, I shall enjoy travelling in Switzerland more than in Germany." Sharp reply: "And what about us, with our *Frente Popular*?"[27] Those few words explain many things. When a Frenchman takes the liberty of expressing his antipathy for the face of Hitler, another Frenchman hastens to suggest that Hitler is better than the men who govern France, and to give more weight to his suggestion, he identifies, mendaciously, the latter with the Spanish revolutionaries.

1938. I am attending a meeting of the contributors to a Paris paper. One of them is upset. There are posters around Paris which trouble him very much. These posters were put up by the Communists. They picture a map of Europe with large arrows pointing menacingly at France. (Let us recall that at this time the Soviet Union had not yet given up its policy of resistance to Nazi Germany.

[27] Spanish expression.

Consequently, the French Communists showed themselves patriotic, even clear-sighted, as you may judge.) These arrows come from Germany, Italy and Spain, in a word from all the countries in which the Nazis had established themselves. Our contributor thought these posters were scandalous and asked that our paper denounce them in the strongest terms. The majority of the editorial board was patriotic and felt little inclined to follow his suggestion. But as the man was a great writer, a very much respected thinker, etc., my colleagues were so weak as to propose that he express his views in the form of a controversy with one of the contributors. And this is how a few weeks after the invasion of Austria and a few months before Munich you could have read in the finest weekly published in Paris, and under the signature of one of the most honored representatives of French thought, that "peace could be endangered only by some imprudence or provocation coming from France."

Must we call this treason?

1938. During the preceding weeks, the newspapers carried sensational revelations about the activities of a gang of conspirators. In Paris and its suburbs several underground arsenals were discovered with stocks of hand grenades, enormous quantities of rifles, revolvers and machine guns. Names are revealed: they are those of members of the Right. There is even among them that of a retired general. These conspirators call themselves: *Secret Committee for Revolutionary Action*, but it is said that they wear hoods (*cagoules*) and newspapers call them *Les Cagoulards*. This word sounds funny and many people are going to exploit it by amusing the public and making it believe that the plot is just a joke. Yet it seems established that this gang is guilty of several assassinations and acts of terrorism as yet unexplained. Gustave Hervé, the old gentleman who last year shouted: *Hurrah for the Germans*, states in his paper that it is a very good thing for French bourgeois to have machine guns in their cellars, so that they will not be massacred like the Spanish bourgeois. Personally—bourgeois or not, I never felt in danger of being massacred by anybody—I am particularly interested in the origin of these machine guns, hand grenades, and revolvers: these weapons come from Germany and Italy. As there is little likelihood that the German and Italian governments acted without any other motive than the humanitarian desire to prevent French bourgeois from being massacred, the affair is perfectly clear to me. The enemies of France wanted to have in France, at their service, not only members of the Academy, journalists, *et al.*, but also an armed gang which, at the right moment, would spread destruction on the pretext of protecting women and children. I discuss the affair with a young staff officer. He agrees with Gustave Hervé and feels a certain gratitude towards these Cagoulards who are ready to protect his wife and daughter in case the Communists might fancy the idea of cutting them to pieces.

I do not know what became of this officer. Perhaps he died on the field of battle. I am sure he was ready to give his life in the defence of his country. This leads me to consider a question which puzzled the whole world. Was the defeat of France due, at least in part, to acts of treason within the army? It seems that the time has not yet come to give this question a definite answer. But the least that can be said is that a good deal of harm was surely done by certain psychological dispositions more subtle than those which command voluntary treason.

The instructors of future officers, in order to give their students a sense of action, describe for them the psychology of the horseman who jumps over a ditch. It is really possible that the horse miss his jump and that horse and rider fall into the ditch. But if the rider wants to increase his chances of success, he must eliminate from his mind the idea of a possible fall. The idea of a possible fall prevents the rider from gripping the horse with his knees, thus making a fall probable, or inevitable, depending upon the width of the ditch. This is an excellent analysis which holds for all cases in which the aims of the action can be attained only through rigorously coordinated, sudden, tense and paroxysmal action. When the course of events is slow, peaceful, admits of leisure, trials, errors and corrections, a certain amount of afterthought and hesitancy is not necessarily fatal to action. But woe to the soldier through whose mind flashes, at the moment the motorized divisions of the enemy advance, the thought that the Jews and Freemasons wanted the war, and that nothing would have happened had not M. Laval been removed from power, that it was the fault of the English, that the victory of France might be the defeat of civilization, etc.

Poor fellows who rest in final sleep on the plains of Northern France and Belgium, or suffer the dreary despair of prison camps, how could you have helped being struck, at the very moment when heroic action called for the supreme tension of your whole being, by the poisoned arrows of irresolution? Many active officers of the army, and a still greater number of reserve officers, had been demoralized in the course of the preceding years by reading infamous papers. The Minister of War forbade reading *L'Humanité*, the Communist paper, in camp, but that is about all he was permitted to forbid. What could be expected, at the critical hour, of a reserve officer who had read *Gringoire* or *Je Suis Partout* every week for several years? That he let himself be killed if ordered to, but surely nothing more.

Yet, the salvation of France required much more.

X

The Deliverance of the World

At times I may have given the impression that French society had almost completely disintegrated in the course of the last few years, and that the military defeat of the French was but the inevitable result of an irreparable decadence. I wish to correct this impression, if necessary. If we consider the history of contemporary France *as a whole*, and give proper importance to the religious movement, to charitable, missionary, scientific, artistic and juridical activities, it is plain that France has remained great. A day will come when the world will recognize in this period of twenty years between victory and defeat, one of the most fruitful periods in French history. Yet at the beginning of this book, I spoke of the state of exhaustion in which the victory of 1918 had left France. This is the proper place to point out, more precisely than I could in the earlier chapters, the real significance of the symptoms of exhaustion to which I referred.

What was exhausted in the France of the last twenty years was the power of generating, maintaining and exalting the collective beliefs which assure simultaneously the strength, the efficiency and the discipline of collective action. In speaking of the psychology of the French during the great economic crisis I used the expression: *Twilight of the Myths*. This expression really holds for the whole period between the victory of 1918 and the defeat of yesterday. There is no reason to believe that the French became worse, absolutely speaking, during these last twenty years. It should even be said that in many respects they became better. But, against the inroads of destructive passions and ideologies, they lacked the protection of an unquestioned system of beliefs, visions and aspirations—in short they lacked the protection of a *myth*. The disappearance of the spirit of the French Revolution dried up for a while, in the soul of the French people, the power that creates myths. *Yet societies which have the initiative of historical movement, the societies which truly make history, are those which are animated by powerful myths.* Because they no longer had any myth, the French had lost the initiative of their own history and the sense of their national destiny. This is what made possible, in my opinion, the formidable machine of betrayal which I have tried to describe in the preceding chapter.

It is fitting to give here some explanation of the concept of *myth*, as elaborated by Georges Sorel in his deservedly famous observations on the development of proletarian organizations.[28] That which gives rise to the theory of the *myth* in Sorel's work is a problem of method. The question is to determine the method to be used in speculation about the future of societies in order to avoid those arbitrary conjectures which experience never confirms. Against the illusions cherished by certain theorists of social science, Sorel maintains that there does not exist, nor can there exist, any scientific means of knowing the future of societies. Constructions which actually shape the future are not those which express the ideas of a scientist on the society

---

[28] Georges Sorel, *Reflections on Violence*, translated by T. E. Hulme, B. W. Huebsch, New York, p. 133ff.

of the future, but those in which societies express their strongest inclinations: "inclinations which recur to the mind with the insistence of instincts in all the circumstances of life; and which give an aspect of complete reality to the hopes of immediate action by which, more easily than by any other method, men can reform their desires, passions and mental activity."

To these visions, these expressions of collective aspirations, Sorel gives the name of *myths*. As examples of myths, he cites the belief of the early Christians in the imminent return of Christ and His visible victory over the pagan world, the political representations which stirred up the enthusiasm of the pioneers of the French Revolution, the ideal of a free and united Italy pursued by Mazzini and his disciples. In each of these cases, historical reality proved at variance with the expectations which had been outlined. Yet, the "myth" had been an historical force of the utmost efficacy: ". . . it may be asked whether the French Revolution was not a much more profound transformation than those dreamed of by the people who, in the eighteenth century, had invented social utopias . . . it can no longer be denied that without Mazzini Italy would never have become a great power, and that he did more for Italian unity than Cavour and all the politicians of his school."

The myth which is of particular importance to Sorel as an interpreter of the labor movement is that of the *general strike*. Unlike the other examples, the myth of the general strike was a thing present at the time Sorel was writing. His observations on this myth contain some general rules for the study of myths in the collective consciousness of societies: ". . . We are not obliged to indulge in lofty reflections, philosophy, history or economics: we are not on the plane of theories and we can remain in the level of observable facts. We have to question men who take a very active part in the real revolutionary movement . . . These men may be deceived about an infinite number of political, economic, or moral questions; but their testimony is decisive, sovereign and irrefutable when it is a question of knowing which one of the ideas most powerfully moves them and their comrades . . . and thanks to which their reason, their hopes and their way of looking at particular facts seem to make but one indivisible unity."

And here is the great misfortune of our time. In the still recent past, the only groups capable of producing powerful myths were those engaged in the most nefarious undertakings. The myth of the universal revolution which assured the triumph of the Bolshevist outburst in Petrograd in October, 1917, defeated the White Armies, held in check the power of the victorious Entente, and has not yet exhausted its possibilities. Twenty-four years after the October Insurrection, it still helps to maintain the domination of the Communist party over the territories which range from the banks of the Vistula river to the Pacific coast. With regard to the Nazi movement, let us recall that when Hitler came to power, many people shook their heads, thinking that a party, whose program was so vague and consisted mostly in emotional utterances, could not help declining as soon as confronted by the difficulties of real politics. People who reasoned this way did not know the theory of myths. The efficacy of a myth does not depend upon the intelligible elaboration of its content, but upon its emotional appeal, upon its capacity to sum up in a compelling way a host of aspirations.

In the world struggle against Nazism and its allies countless men are suffering and dying for a better future. What are the visions which inspire them, inflame their resolutions, console their sufferings? In order to understand the essence of Socialism, Sorel observed men "who take a very active part in the real revolutionary movement"; similarly we will ask what are the supremely efficacious representations of the men most actively engaged in the struggle against Nazi Germany and her allies.

All testimonies agree: soldiers on the firing line, statesmen charged with the heaviest responsibilities, the men in the street subjected to the horrors of bombings, finally and on a very humble level, journalists, writers, orators who pursue the indispensable task of making known the truth about the present-day tragedies,—*all have in mind, not visions of glory nor of power, but visions of freedom.* There is a striking eloquence in the names adopted spontaneously by the survivors of the conquered nations in their continued and obstinate struggle against the conqueror. *Free Poland, Free France*: these expressions do not refer only to the ideal in which every true Frenchman or every true Pole hopes, they refer also to real organisations, actually existing, and suffering,—to groups of men in whom an ideal has become incarnated in suffering bodies and impassioned action, and who, in their suffering and sacrifice, already grasp, already bring into existence that liberation of their country for which they are ready to die.

Furthermore, here is a phenomenon unprecedented in all history: the living and active forces of freedom are uniting citizens of all countries. In the great army of Freedom there are found not only citizens of the countries in open war with the powers of tyranny: citizens of the British Commonwealth of Nations, Americans, Poles, Dutch, Jugoslavs . . . All the countries of the world, including those which are officially governed by the forces of tyranny, are represented in the army of Freedom. There are Free Germans who are fighting for the deliverance of Germany, Free Italians who are fighting for the deliverance of Italy, Free French who are fighting for the deliverance of France. These combatants from all over the world have a common consciousness; the visions of freedom which haunt their minds are converging to form one great vision which will be the victorious myth of the future: *the sublime vision of the liberation of the world.*

A great many people would like to know how the society of tomorrow will be organized, what will be the concrete form of this "better future" for which we are fighting: will capitalism be preserved, abolished, modified, controlled? Will labor relations be established on the basis of contracts between labor and management or on the basis of a guild legislation? What will be the respective parts played in economic life by the principle of exchange and by the principle of free distribution?

THE DELIVERANCE OF THE WORLD 203

We do not doubt the importance of such questions, nor the usefulness of plans and conjectures. But the *essential* thing is the human character, the spirit, the inspiration, the emotional tone of this ensemble of volitions and sacrifices which are summed up in the image of the deliverance of the world.

There are men throughout the world who believe it is most desirable that economic life be subject to bureaucratic regulation, that the souls of children be militarized and thinking be enslaved, that the passions and interests of a party be substituted for the common good of the whole of society, that religion become the tool of a party, *that the Church itself, according to the expression of the Patriarch of Lisbon, be "dechristianized,"* that Jews be outlawed and Negroes reduced again to slavery, that the weak be without any right of appeal against the strong. These men compose the International of Dictatorships and their myth is the *New Order*. Should they triumph, what would be the concrete form of the organization they would impose upon the world? Nobody can describe it accurately, but this we do know, that in such an "order," there would be neither truth nor freedom nor justice.

I shall not try to describe the order which shall be brought about by the victory of the forces of Freedom. The only certain thing (and after all, is it not the all-essential thing?) is that the very nature of these forces will compel them to evolve a world where the principle of equal justice for all will prevail, a world where Jews will have the same rights to justice as Aryans, Negroes the same as Whites, the poor the same as the rich; a world where religion will neither be persecuted, nor corrupted, but free; a world where the word of truth will be free to resound. This is all we have to know and we need know no more than this in order to give our lives.

May the readers of this book consider earnestly the universal bearing of the painful experiences of the French nation. France let herself be corrupted and betrayed, she abandoned herself to corrupters and traitors because the French had no collective beliefs, had no positive ideas, had no inspiring myth. Uncertainty among the French gave the corrupters the benefit of the doubt, the benefit of a tolerant and liberal treatment in the shadow of which was built the *pyramid of treachery* we have described. The first salutary effect that we can expect from the great idea of the liberation of the world is an outburst of uncompromising determination, a singleness of purpose and a vigorous hatred for corruption in all its forms, beginning with the most subtle ones which are the most redoubtable of all.

Once every free man has understood that his will ought to be one with the will of those who give their lives on the battlefield in the fight for freedom; once every free man has understood that the great goal of all free men exacts of each a fervor, a steadiness, a resolution, an anger equal to those which animate the combatants on the battlefields; then the traitors can not pass themselves off, as they did in France,—as nationalists; then the sympathizers with the enemy will cringe with terror, and the irresolute will learn how to overcome their irresolution. Then the smoke-screen behind which the enemy advances will be swept away, then propaganda will no longer play the role of artillery preparation. This will be the beginning of the march to deliverance.

Table of Events

1918 Nov. 11, Armistice.
1919 June 28, Treaty of Versailles.
1919 Nov. 16, Rightist parties win first postwar elections to the Chamber.
1922 April-May, Genoa Conference at which, for the first time since the Peace Treaties, representatives of the victorious Entente meet with delegates of Germany and Soviet Russia. While the Conference was in session, the German and Soviet delegates signed an agreement at Rapallo.
1923 Jan., Occupation of the Ruhr district by the French armies.
1923 Nov. 8, Hitler's putsch in Munich fails.
1923 Dec., Electoral victory of the Labor Party in Britain. The first Labor government was formed early in 1924.
1924 May 11, Electoral triumph of the Leftist Coalition (Cartel des Gauches).
1924 Aug., London Conference. Evacuation of the Ruhr

decided. The Allies and Germany adopt the Dawes Plan with regard to Reparations.

1925 Oct., Pact of Locarno.

1926 Sept. 5, Letter of Pope Pius XI approving the letter by which Cardinal Andrieu exhorted French Catholic youth to keep away from the *Action Française*.

1926 Dec. 20, *L'Action Française* put on the Index.

1929 Oct. 9, Death of Stresemann, the German signatory of the Pact of Locarno.

1930 Sept., Nazis make startling gains at elections (from 12 to 107 deputies out of a total of 577).

1931 Sept., Japan starts the invasion of Manchuria.

1933 Jan., Hitler becomes Chancellor.

1934 Feb. 6, French political crisis reaches climax in bloody riots in Paris.

1935 Jan., Plebiscite in the Saar. Return of Saar district to German sovereignty.

1935 Oct., Italo-Ethiopian war begins.

1936 Feb., People's Front comes into power in Spain.

1936 March 7, Remilitarization of the Rhineland (Treaty of Locarno scrapped).

1936 May, People's Front wins French elections.

1936 June, Sit-down strikes in France.

1936 July, General Franco revolts; beginning of Civil War in Spain.

1938 March, Anschluss of Austria and Germany. Soon afterwards, Rightist papers begin to advocate the appeasement of Nazi Germany.

1938 May, New cabinet headed by Daladier. End of People's Front regime.

1938 Sept. 30, Munich Agreement.